Living the Victory

Living the Victory

God's Strategies for Spiritual Warfare

JERE PROBERT

LIVING THE VICTORY
GOD'S STRATEGIES FOR SPIRITUAL WARFARE

All scripture used in this book is from the New American Standard Bible unless it is identified differently.

iUniverse books may be ordered through booksellers or by contacting:

iUniverse
1663 Liberty Drive
Bloomington, IN 47403
www.iuniverse.com
1-800-Authors (1-800-288-4677)

ISBN: 978-1-4917-6502-9 (sc)
ISBN: 978-1-4917-6501-2 (e)

Print information available on the last page.

iUniverse rev. date: 04/21/2015

Contents

Preface

This book is an effort to scripturally define and clarify the basics of spiritual warfare in layman's terms. It was prompted by attending a home Bible study that used purchased material. The study was of little spiritual, intellectual, or practical value. There was no clarification of what God planned or what Jesus accomplished with His life, death, and resurrection.

Spiritual warfare is a reality. Of that I am sure. I am also certain that there is not a demon behind every doorknob as some teachers would have you believe.

Having been a born-again follower of Jesus for some forty years, one fact has become obvious to me. That fact is that we Christians do not display the power of God to the heathen nations very well. Nonbelievers can't tell the difference between our lives and theirs. We don't display the power of God to one another very well either! We need to look at a couple of word pictures from the Bible to see what God's followers should look like to the rest of the world.

One of the major problems I encounter when teaching spiritual warfare to believers revolves around the Holy Spirit and perceptions of Him. When I talk about Satan, people seem to visualize a militaristic organizational structure. They seem to understand the devil as the leader of a band of outlaws, like in an old Hollywood western movie.

But that changes when I introduce the good guys from that old movie script. It is as if they can only see the sheriff. The main good guy is the Holy Spirit, and He doesn't need a posse. Problems develop when I scripturally introduce God's response by listing spirits that are identified by the work they do in God's kingdom. Though they are acknowledged in it, this is not a book about angels.

Two passages help me explain what I call the "helping" spirits, those who are helping the Holy Spirit.

> The angel answered and said to me, "These are the four spirits of heaven, going forth after standing before the Lord of all the earth, with one of which the black horses are going forth to the north country; and the white ones go forth after them, while the dappled ones go forth to the south country. When the strong ones went out, they were eager to go to patrol the earth." And He said, "Go, patrol the earth." So they patrolled the earth. Then He cried out to me and spoke to me saying, "See, those who are going to the land of the north have appeased my wrath in the land of the north." (Zechariah 6:5–8)

Zechariah is presented with a vision. These verses explain the vision. He is told that the vision is of the four spirits of heaven sent forth. Verse 8 explains that they have appeased God's wrath. They did what they were told to do. Verse 7, in the Amplified and some other translations, says that their works have "quieted My Spirit." The capital letters tell us that it is the Holy Spirit's wrath being quieted by the work of those four. That is why I call them helping spirits.

The second example demonstrating this principle is from Revelation 5.

> I saw between the throne (with the four living creatures) and the elders a Lamb standing, as if slain, having seven horns and seven eyes, which are the seven Spirits of God, sent out into all the earth. (Revelation 5:6)

This verse again demonstrates the existence of spirit beings that are part of the heavens. These, like the four in Zechariah, are being sent out into the earth. This book scripturally identifies different helping spirits—usually biblical examples of their activities and the outcomes of their interventions on behalf of God's people. There are many of these spirits empowered by God to assist His people to be overcomers.

I have used the New American Standard Bible as my primary text in this book. Variations from that are clearly identified.

Unit 1

Introduction—A Historical Perspective

Chapter 1 of the book of Joshua starts with God telling Joshua several times that he needs to be courageous and strong. God says that He will be with Joshua, that He will not fail him nor forsake him. Having that promise from God should make it easier for anyone to be courageous and strong! You would think that following a God who displayed Himself as a pillar of fire by night and a pillar of smoke every day for forty years would make His promise totally believable.

In Joshua 2:9, Rahab said to the men, "I know that the Lord has given you the land, and that the terror of you has fallen on us, and that all the inhabitants of the land, those of us who have lived here for generations have melted away before you."

The phrase "melted away" can be translated as "become demoralized." These Gentiles, these people of the world, had observed the power with the Israelites from the day they left Egypt. They were afraid of them. People of the world, the heathens, the Gentiles no longer melt away or "become demoralized" in the presence of God's people.

Taking prayer out of schools is an example of powerless Christianity in society today. When Rahab was speaking those words ("melted away"), it was because she saw her people cowering in fear or terror of God's people. In Joshua 2:24, we are told again that the heathens are in terror of God's people.

> They said to Joshua, "Surely the Lord has given all the land into our hands; moreover, all the inhabitants of the land have melted away before us." (Joshua 2:24)

Given the attitude of the inhabitants of Rahab's land, do you think they would have the courage to say to Joshua, "While you are here, we will not allow you to pray in the schools"? Of course they wouldn't say that to God's people. They had seen the power of God.

The Amplified and King James translations of scripture use the term "faint" instead of "melt away." In this account, the nation finds itself at odds with God's people. It has seen the power of God demonstrated on behalf of His people. They have seen the pillar of fire by night and the cloud by day. They have heard how He crushed opposition from neighboring kings.

They have seen His people thriving in spite of the odds against them. As the original inhabitants of the land, they have good reason to fear the God of the Israelites. God gave their nation to His own people. They were told to possess it. They did possess it. They were overcomers.

We have been called to be overcomers. By being an overcomer, I am referring to a person who willing and joyfully takes possession of that which God through His grace has allocated to him/her. An example would be His promise that whoever believes in His son, Jesus Christ, should not perish but have everlasting life. An overcomer takes possession of that gift.

Do we look like, act like, or speak like anything in our lives has been overcome? Do we look like, act like, or speak like we serve and belong to the God of Abraham, Isaac, or Jacob? Do we look like, act like, or speak like we serve and belong to the God of Peter, Paul, and John?

We have been called to proudly live and walk in a victorious faith. How are we doing? Is it possible to walk with God in victory? Within this study, we'll be looking at how to do that.

Today's world does not see people walking with the God of power. Has this world ever seen that sort of thing? Absolutely.

At the end of World War II, remaining Japanese leaders reportedly told General Douglas MacArthur of the U.S. Army that it was obvious the God of America was greater than their god. They then reportedly asked for teachings about Him. A devout Episcopalian, MacArthur called upon a group of evangelicals, saying, "Japan is a spiritual vacuum. If you do not fill it with Christianity, it will be filled with Communism. Send me 1,000 missionaries." He asked US missionary societies to send "Bibles, Bibles, and more Bibles." MacArthur spoke freely, saying that postwar Japan was in a spiritual vacuum. All previous "gods" had failed—its invincible military, its divine emperor, its thousand-year belief that the Land of the Rising Sun would rule the world. Now the conquered people of Japan had nothing.

> "Today it is virtually unthinkable in our politically correct world to imagine a U.S. president or American general asking for missionaries or bibles to be sent as part of a foreign aid program. Yet following Japan's surrender at the end of WWII, five-star General Douglas MacArthur remained in Japan to help rebuild its governmental system. A devout Episcopalian, MacArthur said to a visiting group of evangelicals that "Japan is a spiritual vacuum. Send me 1,000 missionaries." Famously, General MacArthur asked U.S. missionary societies to send "Bibles, Bibles and more Bibles." Sadly, General MacArthur's call for missionaries and Bibles for Japan went largely unheeded. (MercyWorks, "NOW is Japan's Hour," http://mercyworks.org/asia/japan/now-is-japan%E2%80%99s-hour/)

Unfortunately, the rest of that story does not end the way we believers would like. It seems the missionary infiltration didn't happen as MacArthur asked. Since they didn't have the spiritual input they needed, the Japanese observed us. They saw a land that appeared to have gods they understood: money, efficiency, and hard work. Instead of the God of Israel, they adopted the gods of America.

The whole book of Acts is a New Testament account that supports the idea that unbelievers ought to fear God and His people. Acts 5 tells the account of a husband and wife who lied to the church leadership and thereby to the Holy Spirit—they died immediately. The result was that a fear came upon the believers and everyone who heard about it.

> And great fear came over the whole church, and over all who heard of these things. (Acts 5:11)

What about us? What about now? The scriptures haven't changed. They still tell us we are to overcome. What has changed in these many years since World War II ended? Have we as a nation changed?

> And they overcame him because of the blood of the Lamb and because of the word of their testimony, and they did not love their life even when faced with death. (Revelation 12:11)

> For whatever is born of God overcomes the world; and this is the victory that has overcome the world—our faith. (1 John 5:4)

Those scriptures still speak the truth. It is believers in this country that have changed. We have allowed idolatry. Instead of telling the Japanese about the God who created all things, we showed them how we made automobiles.

What I am observing today is a pseudo-Christianity, where the individual Christian is hard to distinguish from the run-of-the-mill heathen walking the street. This American does good works, gives to charity, and pays his bills but doesn't glorify or honor the God who empowered him to succeed. This same "good works" mind-set leads to churches that are hard to distinguish from country clubs. That is not what Jesus died for.

> For assuredly He does not give help to angels, but He gives help to the descendants of Abraham. Therefore, He had to be made like His brethren in all things, so that He might become a merciful and faithful high priest in things pertaining to God, to make propitiation for the sins of the people. For since He Himself was tempted in that which He has suffered, He is able to come to the aid of those who are tempted. (Hebrews 2:16–18)

"Propitiation" means perfect sacrifice. Jesus became the only possible perfect sacrifice for my sins and for your sins. It didn't end there either. This unbelievable supernatural payment gave us access by the Son of God to the Creator God. These facts and their meaning are what equip us to be overcomers! Jesus gave us access to God. We are redeemed! He died for our redemption.

> However, the Law is not of faith; on the contrary, "He who practices them shall live by them." Christ redeemed us from the curse of the Law, having become a curse for us—for it is written, "Cursed is everyone who hangs on a tree" in order that in Christ Jesus the blessing of Abraham might come to the Gentiles, so that we would receive the promise of the Spirit through faith. (Galatians 3:12–14)

> [It instructs] us to deny ungodliness and worldly desires and to live sensibly, righteously and godly in the present age, looking for the blessed hope and the appearing of the glory of our great God and Savior, Christ Jesus, who gave Himself for us to redeem us from every lawless deed, and to purify for Himself a people for His own possession, zealous for good deeds. (Titus 2:12–14)

We have been bought, redeemed, and delivered from the kingdom of darkness to the kingdom of light. This spiritual transaction was accomplished by the Son of the Living God. If He is so firmly on our side, why are we so hard to distinguish from the world? What are we missing? Why do we feel as if we sometimes have to make excuses for God?

Jesus died to gain victory over the enemy, and He was successful. Just as His Father promised the Israelites victory in possessing their land of "milk and honey," Jesus took away the power of our enemy. But like God's people in the old covenant, we seem unable or unwilling to do the possessing. We have to learn to make victory in daily life ours. We must possess it. We have not learned to live in the life He has prepared for us.

> … Having canceled out the certificate of debt consisting of decrees against us, which was hostile to us; and He has taken it out of the way, having nailed it to the cross. When He had disarmed the rulers and authorities, He

made a public display of them, having triumphed over them through Him. (Colossians 2:14–15)

… Which He brought about in Christ, when He raised Him from the dead and seated Him at His right hand in the heavenly places, far above all rule and authority and power and dominion, and every name that is named, not only in this age but also in the one to come. And He put all things in subjection under His feet, and gave Him as head over all things to the church. (Ephesians 1:20–22)

Sin was defeated at the cross, and everything became subject to Jesus when the Father raised Him from the dead. Understanding the completeness of Jesus's victory is essential to being an effective spiritual warrior.

Much of Christianity and Christian behavior is difficult to distinguish from that of the non-Christian world. The value systems displayed and the behaviors demonstrated reflect more of the fallen world than of the risen Savior. In the Bible, Paul calls this type of living, "holding to a form of godliness while denying the power thereof." He meant that we can claim to live godly lives but deny the power of God—deny that we need to live as though we're different from nonbelievers.

But realize this, that in the last days difficult times will come. For men will be lovers of self, lovers of money, boastful, arrogant, revilers, disobedient to parents, ungrateful, unholy, unloving, irreconcilable, malicious gossips, without self-control, brutal, haters of good, treacherous, reckless, conceited, lovers of pleasure rather than lovers of God, holding to a form of godliness, although they have denied its power; avoid such men as these. (2 Timothy 3:1–5)

In his second letter, Peter referred to people who live that way as being like springs without water (2 Peter 2:17). My observation is that a spring without water does not fulfill the function for which it was created. Any follower of the Messiah must understand the authority structure of the universe. If that understanding of authority is not in the innermost being of a person, success in spiritual warfare will be more a matter of luck than of faith. We become like blind squirrels hunting for acorns. There may be a little occasional success, but it won't be consistent.

I cringe when I hear a believer credit unspeakably bad things to God and attempt to sound religiously wise while saying it. God's Word says due to lack of knowledge His people will not flourish. See Hosea 4:7.

Romans 10:17 tells us that faith—our belief system about the kingdom *of* heaven—comes from the repeated hearing of the Word of God. That is my personal translation of the verse. Unfortunately, our belief system can easily buy into a lie or false doctrine we hear over and over from people we trust. It must deeply grieve God's Holy Spirit to see churches full of religious patrons proclaiming unscriptural thinking based on worldly political correctness.

Speaking in the natural world, it would be hard to imagine the citizens of any nation fighting a war and not knowing they were at war. Usually the warriors are equipped by the government and esteemed by the people. In America, we say they are fighting for our freedom. Perhaps all of this makes you wonder what I think we believers should look like to the world and how we should impact them. Is the Church of today actively equipping their own people—or even holding them in high esteem?

This study is designed to scripturally define the spiritual war that many Christians choose to ignore. God will clearly show how we can be visible overcomers. It is possible for us today to look much more like God's people did in Joshua 2 and Acts 5.

Discussion Topics from Unit 1

According to Hebrews 2:16–18, for what did Jesus die?

According to Galatians 3:12–14, for what did Jesus die?

According to Colossians 2:14 and 15, what two things happened at the cross?

According to Ephesians 1:20–22, what happened when God raised Jesus from the dead?

Define the word "redeem":

Unit 2

Beginning of the Beginning

Is our desire to walk with the Lord as overcomers on this earth? Assuming it is, then we must have a clear view of the sequence of events from the beginning and the impact of those events on how things are today. We need to know what God created. Though it sounds too simple when one says it, He created all things.

We need to know that Lucifer got himself booted out of God's presence. We need to know that man fell from grace. He sold out his God-given dominion over the planet. We need to know that Jesus Christ redeemed us and bought us back. We need to know that the Holy Spirit indwells us and empowers us.

Spiritual warfare is a battle for our very soul and spirit. Satan would like to eventually see us in hell with him. When we have become children of God, that plan of the devil won't work. His next best ploy is to disempower us in the here and now. He wants us out of the battle on earth. In a practical sense, if we are in heaven, we are not bothering him here. So let's get started with beginning at the beginning.

We are going to find the beginning in the book of Genesis. We'll look at what mankind's relationship with his Creator and his environment was before the fall. There we will find what I consider the best, if not the only, example of the relationship with man that God intended when He created them (man and woman). We were designed to be in fellowship with Him, and we were designed to be in obedience to Him. We were designed to have responsibilities assigned by Him, and we were designed to fulfill those responsibilities assigned by Him. Genesis 1 is where we will start working our way through this word picture God gave us.

> Then God said, "Let Us make man in Our image, according to Our likeness; and let them rule over the fish of the sea and over the birds of the sky and over the cattle and over all the earth, and over every creeping thing that creeps on the earth." (Genesis 1:26–31)

In the beginning, Man was created: pure, holy, loving, and righteous. How do we know that? Because he was created in God's image, with God's characteristics—he was created like God. This last creation, this man, was to do what? Man and woman were to rule over all the earth. All the earth—nothing in it needed to be redeemed!

There was nothing there that God considered unclean. This sovereign God gave mankind, who was His crowning creation, dominion over earth, which was His creation. Genesis 1:27 echoes verse 26.

> God created man in His own image, in the image of God He created him; male and female He created them. (Genesis 1:27)

This looks like a clarification verse. His definition of the word "man" changed to "male and female" between those two verses. Galatians 3 seems to endorse this thought of a spiritual position of oneness or lack of gender in the spirit. Paul calls us all "sons." When it comes to being a child of God, gender differences seem irrelevant.

Looking once more in Genesis 1:28, we find another blessing. Reading through verse 31, we get a sense of how total this blessing was as well as how much responsibility came with the blessing.

> God blessed them; and God said to them, "Be fruitful and multiply, and fill the earth, and subdue it; and rule over the fish of the sea and over the birds of the sky and over every living thing that moves on the earth." (Genesis 1:28)

Examine the responsibility God gave man. First, He blessed them. My definition of "to bless" is "to empower to succeed." Then He gave them authority "to rule over" the earth.

In the King James version, the words "rule over" are translated to have "dominion over." This dominion over, or responsibility and accountability for, the earth clearly is given to man and woman.

> Then God said, "Behold, I have given you every plant yielding seed that is on the surface of all the earth, and every tree which has fruit yielding seed; it shall be food for you." (Genesis 1:29)

God then defines what this means. He says all these systems are equipped to be eternally self-sustaining.

> And to every beast of the earth and to every bird of the sky and to every thing that moves on the earth which has life, I have given every green plant for food. (Genesis 1:30)

Everything He has created can reproduce itself, and there is a food chain to support everything. All of creation was created to be self-perpetuating. God did not intend to have to create again or establish a further support system for His completed creation.

> God saw all that He had made, and behold, it was very good. And there was evening and there was morning, the sixth day. (Genesis 1:31)

His blessing was and still is empowerment to succeed. His blessing was all they needed. He liked His creation. He said it was very good.

Discussion Topics from Unit 2

According to Genesis 1:26, in whose image were we created?

According to Genesis 1:28, what did God give to man?

According to Genesis 1:31, what did God say about His finished creation?

According to Isaiah 14:14, what did Satan say he would do for himself?

According to Genesis 2:17, what would happen to Adam and Eve if they didn't get it right?

Unit 3

The Performance Triangle

Man and woman were given complete charge of the system God created. The Bible says that God gave them dominion. Notice that He gave man and woman a responsibility. Obviously He expected them to perform or fulfill that responsibility.

He gave them authority to perform those tasks for which they were responsible. When a job is given to a person, that job is a responsibility. With the responsibility must come the authority and tools to do the job. The final side of that triangle of performance is accountability.

Rebellion is sin! There are three major triggers for rebellion in natural man: authority, responsibility, and accountability.

Authority, that first side of the triangle, says there is an entity in charge. The word "authority" is enough to disturb most teenagers. The problem starts long before the teen years and can last a lifetime. A world without authority is anarchy; it is chaos. Some translations of the Bible use the word "chaos" for the condition from which God spoke the universe into being. Interestingly, most of us like authority if we are the ones who have it. We rebel when we are subject to it.

Responsibility: responsibility alludes to having a task to accomplish. It usually includes the tools needed to perform the task. Sometimes the tools are included with the delegation of authority. For example, if someone tells or asks you to change a baby's diaper, they should be furnishing the baby and the fresh diaper. At this point, the authority and responsibility have been delegated. They have been delegated to someone by someone with more authority.

Accountability involves the examination of the outcome of a delegated task. To be held accountable means someone is checking the outcome. Usually there are penalties or rewards based on outcomes. That is true in the natural world or the kingdom of God. It is simple to ascertain if a baby that needed changing experienced that act. It is not always that easy.

In 2001, I was hired as director for a program called Family Development and Self-Sufficiency. The program was statewide and was one of the state of Iowa's responses to the Welfare to Work law. It was an in-home empowerment concept that worked with chronically, inter-generationally unemployed. The area I was to direct covered seven counties in NE Iowa. I was told those seven counties covered an area bigger than the state of Delaware. The program had been without a director for months. As a result of this period without anyone in charge (no one in authority), it was not in good standing with the state funding agency. It had become disorganized in terms of reports, record keeping, and general housekeeping.

My first action was to identify all time sensitive required reports, those for which I would be held accountable. I printed signs on 8½ × 11–inch paper. Each sign started with the words: "If you want this job, such and such report must be filed by …" Then I inserted the correct date for that report. I posted the signs on the wall so I could see them anytime. I had the job and the tools. I had the authority. I had to provide my own accountability on a day-by-day basis. My supervisor certainly planned to hold me accountable at the end of the year. I understood how the triangle worked, and the outcomes were satisfactory.

The New Testament gives a biblical example of God clearly assigning jobs to His people. In Ephesians, it says that He has appointed some as teachers whose job is to equip the saints. The appointment and the purpose—that is, the authority, the responsibility, and tools—are set out in chapter 4, verses 11 and 12. The various offices listed here are set apart, anticipating an outcome. The outcome (responsibility) of their work was to be the equipping of the saints. We need to look elsewhere for the accountability for the performance of the job.

In Ephesians 4:11 and 12, He gave the order.

> And He gave some as apostles, and some as prophets, and
> some as evangelists, and some as pastors and teachers, for

the equipping of the saints for the work of service, to the building up of the body of Christ. (Ephesians 4:11–12)

God also gave these equippers a couple of divine tools to help them. He gave them the scriptures and the Holy Spirit. Those tools are unquestionably adequate to perform the task. I am also just as certain that Adam and Eve were well equipped to "rule over" or to have dominion over planet Earth. They had the Creator walking with them. They didn't have the book; they had the Author.

Adam and Eve had a job or responsibility, and He gave them authority to perform those tasks for which they were responsible. They had the authority and tools to perform it. Accountability was unbelievable. It was, "If you don't get this right, you shall surely die." The accountability for the New Testament equippers is nearly as strong. We find it in verse 1 of Luke 17.

He said to His disciples, "It is inevitable that stumbling blocks come, but woe to him through whom they come! It would be better for him if a millstone were hung around his neck and he were thrown into the sea, than that he would cause one of these little ones to stumble." (Luke 17:1–2)

Have you ever been in a position or a job where you were not given the authority or the tools needed to perform the job? When this happens, a person is held accountable for outcomes that he doesn't have the ability to affect. I spent several years on local and regional school boards. School boards are elected to oversee the education of our children. We all agree on that. They should be held accountable for the outcome. We all agree on that as well. However, occasionally the state restricts the actions that boards can take to change behaviors of employees or students. The authority of the board of directors as boss is gone. Often this results in anger and chaos. Another thing that might limit the authority of a board would be to mandate a change without paying for it. In other words, the Department of Education might mandate a change within schools but not fund the cost of it. It is difficult to be held accountable for an outcome when you are without authority or the tool needed to succeed. In that case, money was the tool.

God doesn't work that way. When He assigns responsibility, He does it the right way. He made that clear from the start. Adam and Eve were provided with everything they needed to make Eden work. There was only one rule or law from God.

New Testament believers have the provisions needed to meet God's expectations. In Luke 17, God said we are going to be held accountable. Then he said offenders would be better off to have a millstone around their neck and be thrown into the sea than to mess it up! Those of us who have been given one or more of those gifts should have a healthy, respectful fear of He who gave us these gifts.

For example, if I am correctly teaching from the scripture on the deity of Jesus, and my student chooses to deny the identity of Jesus as fact, who is accountable for that? Yes, it is a bad outcome or stumbling block, but it would not be my responsibility to do anything further than teach to the best of my ability based on knowledge of the Word. Teachers are empowered by God to teach the truth, but we are not empowered to make anyone accept it. That would be exceeding the authority given and beyond the responsibility delegated; therefore the teacher will not be held accountable, but rather the student will be.

The reverse of that would be a teacher creating a stumbling block for his students by teaching a "doctrine of demons." That refers to any teaching that is in opposition to Jesus's true self or that speaks incorrect things about the Word of God. Any teaching that opposes scripture is wrong. That wrong teacher will be held accountable for poor performance of his or her job in the kingdom. That teacher would be guilty of incorrectly using the authority and wrongly discharging the responsibility of his position. There is a righteous and holy approach to the performance triangle. Obviously the above example does not hold up to those standards.

According to His Word, God's appointed ones are to be building up the body of Christ, not leading it to harm. I knew a young man who seriously questioned if he was called to the ministry because of the millstone threat (Luke 17:1). I considered him to be a wise young man. He was thinking about seeking God's authority and responsibility with caution. He was counting the cost before making the decision. He did become a minister and is approaching the end of a career as a minister. This example is that of a wise and righteous approach to God. What happens if you don't consider what God is saying? We know what happened when man chose to disobey God in the beginning. We have just been looking at what happens in the present if we don't do our assigned job His way. In all cases, disobedience to God is sin!

I am going to relate a true account of what it is like when mankind decides righteousness is not necessary. A bad decision can result when a person decides to forsake the good teaching that has been part of his life. The outcome is the same as for the person who has been subject to poor teaching or no teaching. The spiritual battle is in the head, in the decision-making part of our being. When one decides to follow what he knows rather than what God knows he is headed for a danger zone.

I was privy to a conversation between two recovering addicts named Bob and Dan. Bob had been raised in a Bible-believing family. Bob chose to ignore what was being taught. Dan had been a victim of poor teaching or no teaching. They were sharing with some believers concerning the real, almost tangible presence of evil when they were in drug-related activities. For them, there was a thrill or rush of some sort in the experience of doing something they inherently knew to be wrong. As they told it, their countenances changed. It was as if they were having trouble believing what they had willfully done. They had allowed themselves to enter an atmosphere where any and all demonic spirits were welcome. The demonic presence was palatable. Have you experienced anything like that? What did it seem like to you? How did that presence of evil get here and get so powerful? One might add, "And what were you doing there?"

In light of the Genesis verses we read earlier where God said of His creation, "It was very good," the questions become: How did this planet, which God once called "very good," become a place where evil is so readily accessible? And how do we fight it or protect ourselves from the force that made evil so readily available? And finally, who is the boss here? We need to know this because this is where our hope is and where our victory is.

There are two opposite cosmic forces at odds with each other on this earth. Who is in the middle? We are! We don't have to be trapped there; we don't have to get caught. We do have a choice about staying there. That snare is broken! Praise God we don't have to think the enemy has us trapped right where we are. What is at stake for us? Our now and our forever are at stake.

Any time I get involved in a discussion with people who feel trapped, I am reminded of Psalm 124.

> Our soul has escaped as a bird out of the snare of the trapper; the snare is broken and we have escaped. (Psalm 124:7)

The word "snare" fits with exactly how the enemy likes to work. He loves a well-disguised trap located in a place where the victim is known to hang out. When the unsuspecting victims step in the snare, it closes on them in such a way that they cannot release themselves. Praise God that snare is broken. I have a story I like to tell that demonstrates how we Christians respond to the fact that the snare is broken. I named this story "The Tale of the Hypnotized Chicken."

I grew up on a Midwestern general farm. The farm had several different kinds of livestock, including about two hundred laying hens. Every year, early in the spring, my parents bought baby chicks, so there were always laying hens in the chicken coop. These hens could and would spend their summer days scratching around in the dirt, usually staying within several hundred feet of their coop. As a result of their activity, their home was surrounded by lots of dust.

Couple this setup with some boys, an isolated farm, the Second World War, and a total lack of entertainment beyond a battery-operated radio, and you have an opportunity for creativity. One of the boys was told that it is possible to hypnotize a chicken, and we had to test it out.

We had been told to hold the captured chicken's wings tight to its side and place her belly down on the dusty ground. Having achieved this, we held her head and neck tight to the dust, straight out in front of her body. At this point, one boy was pretty much occupied, both hands and both feet. The next step was to slowly draw a line in the dust from the point of the hen's beak straight for about two feet. A second boy was required to complete this part of the entertainment. After a few repetitions of that exercise, the hen—who was totally engrossed in the activity—could be released and would lie there in the dust watching the line being drawn. In a few more minutes, the two boys could walk away, and she would lie there staring at that line. Sometimes the hen would lie there so long we would get bored and leave her lying there. There was no snare. She was totally free but would lie in the dust convinced she could not move.

Sound like someone you know? There is a decision that needs to be made. Are you going to lie in the dirt and dust, totally immobilized? Are you going to get up and stomp around, clucking? Or are you going to get up and do something positive? Spiritual warfare starts in the head. Jesus indeed broke the snare of the enemy. Any time the enemy can get us to think we are better off lying in the dust, he has won a round in the fight.

Satan has a mission statement and a strategic plan, and it is not within that plan that any soul should escape! Satan's mission statement is to be bigger and more powerful than God.

Satan's strategic plan is to separate mankind from God, now and forever. He wants our soul destined to be with him in anguish forever—forever separated from God, forever in torment. The story of Dan and Bob shows just how successful Satan has been. It shows just how vulnerable we have become.

The good news is that what I told you is just the first half of the story. Although Bob and Dan did not know each other and were half a continent away from each other when they were operating in the domain of Satan, they both ended up in a jail. In their jail cells, they trusted their future to the Lordship of Jesus Christ. They decided what God promised them is far superior to what Satan offered. They are now both clean and living productive lives, productive for the body of Christ and for society.

This war we are in is fought in our heads. It has physical manifestations that show up after the battle has been fought. We have to decide to accept the tools and instructions God has made available to us. We must understand our tools, our responsibility, and our authority.

Discussion Topics from Unit 3

According to Ephesians 4:11, list the job opportunities in the kingdom of God:

According to Ephesians 4:12, what is the common purpose of the offices listed in the previous verse?

According to Luke 17:1, what are sure to come?

According to Psalm 124:7, what happened to the enemy's snare and what do we have?

According to Isaiah 14:14, what did Satan say he would do for himself?

Unit 4

How the Trouble Started

In the book of Luke, chapter 10, Jesus had sent out seventy of His followers to prepare the way for Him. They returned in triumph. Everything must have gone their way. In today's English, what they reported would have sounded like, "Man, even those demons do what we tell them when we tell them who sent us." In the next verse, Jesus begins to explain the history of spiritual warfare and why Satan obeyed the command of Jesus people using Jesus's name.

> And He said to them, "I was watching Satan fall from heaven like lightning." (Luke 10:18)

Satan and Jesus had been together for eternity. They had lived with God. Satan knew Jesus to be the Son of God. Satan knew—and still knows—that at the name of Jesus, every knee is going to bow. We are the ones who seem to have forgotten that.

Jesus, who has always existed, is proclaiming a truth in this verse. He makes the statement so simple and straightforward that it becomes hard to understand. It is a bit of His testimony. He is saying, "I was there. I saw it. I saw the battle in heaven, and I saw the outcome. I am telling you there can be no doubt that Satan fell from grace in heaven."

Let's bear that in mind while we look at what Isaiah said in chapter 14.

> How you have fallen from heaven, O star of the morning,
> son of the dawn! You have been cut down to the earth,

you who have weakened the nations! But you said in your heart, "I will ascend to heaven; I will raise my throne above the stars of God, and I will sit on the mount of assembly in the recesses of the north. I will ascend above the heights of the clouds; I will make myself like the Most High." Nevertheless you will be thrust down to Sheol, to the recesses of the pit. (Isaiah 14:12–15)

This Isaiah scripture is an account of Satan's fall from heaven to earth (see verse 12) with the ultimate destination of the "sheol" to the recesses of the pit. Notice all the "I will" statements in these few verses. Five times in thirteen short lines, Satan says, "I will."

I will ascend to heaven …

I will raise a throne where I want it.

I will sit on the mount …

I will be higher than the clouds in the spiritual realm.

I will make myself just like God.

They are rebellious statements, not obedient ones. Satan's intent was to be like God or even above God in the universe that God had created. These are boastful, prideful statements that reflect a rebellious heart. They are statements that in essence say, "I know better than God." Pride is often a precursor to sin. Rebellion is a sin. Rebellion is a choice, just as all sin is a choice.

One of our modern manifestations of this attitude of sin is now known as the entitlement mind-set. Instead of saying, "I will have a throne higher than God's," we now have a mind-set that says, "I deserve it. I am entitled to it." When a person makes such a statement to God, that person (or angel, in the case of Lucifer) is headed for a fall. As they used to say in the movies, "Them's fightin' words, mister."

God will not tolerate rebellion. Chapter 12 of the book of Revelation addresses the result of the manifestation of the sin of pride as well. Lucifer must have been a power, because it seemed to be a major battle to just throw him out. It cost the life of the Son of God to disempower him on earth.

And there was war in heaven, Michael and his angels waging war with the dragon. The dragon and his angels waged war. (Revelation 12:7)

Satan is remarkably confident. It is generally accepted that he took the angels who agreed with him and started a war with the Creator of the universe. The enemy has angels—perhaps ex-angels is more correct! The battle isn't against Satan alone. He has an army. The battle Michael and the angels are waging for God is taking place in the dominion of heaven. That is where it started, but it ended up with evil relegated to earth, as Jesus witnessed. This is where the devil and his company await their ultimate destination. Revelation 12:9 confirms what Jesus and Isaiah said in verses we looked at earlier.

> And the great dragon was thrown down, the serpent of old who is called the Devil and Satan, who deceives the whole world; he was thrown down to the earth, and his angels were thrown down with him. (Revelation 12:9)

Notice the tense of this verse. The old serpent, he that is called the devil and Satan, the deceiver has long since been relegated or confined to earth. God did not intend for man to live in an evil environment. Man was not equipped to live under these conditions. We now find humans, who were created in the image of God, who were created righteous beings, cohabiting earth in the company of the devil and his minions. They had been thrown out of the company of a righteous God. This planet was meant to be under the dominion of man. During this moment in time, such is not the case. We have a "little g" god ruling over this earth.

In order to review how God wanted it to be, let's go back to Genesis again.

> And God said, "Let Us make man in Our image, after Our likeness; and let them have dominion over the fish of the sea, and over the fowl of the air, and over the cattle, and over all the earth, and over every creeping thing that creepeth upon the earth." Genesis 1:26 KJV

God created the earth and gave man and woman dominion over it. It was theirs, and they were His. But suddenly they find themselves cohabiting with evil. Some would make the case that mankind empowered evil when deciding to agree with Lucifer. The thinking behind this theology goes something like this:

Satan could only present a proposition to Adam and Eve. When they accepted his deal, they gave him the power. They had, as we have today, a choice. The choice is always to agree with God or to agree with Satan. By agreeing with him, they empowered him. Satan's effort to get mankind to follow his will is at the heart of spiritual warfare. The fact that man had been given free will makes the situation even more difficult. God's desire has always been to have people trusting, honoring, and praising Him because they have chosen to believe Him. Men and women have always been free to obey or not obey. Those decisions have either a consequence or reward.

Discussion Topics from Unit 4

According to Luke 10:18, what did Jesus see?

Where was He when He saw it?

Who else was there?

According to Revelation 12:7, what is going on?

According to Revelation 12:9, who gets sent where?

Unit 5

God Cursed the Earth

Note: I am compelled to document to the best of my ability who is in charge of this world. There will be many who disagree with this concept because it appears to be counter to the doctrine of the sovereignty of God.

To remind us how humanity's believing Satan turned out, look at Genesis 3 once more.

> And unto Adam he said, "Because thou hast hearkened unto the voice of thy wife, and hast eaten of the tree, of which I commanded thee, saying, Thou shall not eat of it: cursed is the ground for thy sake; in toil shall thou eat of it all the days of thy life …" (Genesis 3:17 KJV)

Adam and Eve decided to follow Satan. They did so by deciding to believe the devil rather than believe God. The devil now became the embodiment of evil on the earth. It became Satan's domain. Second Corinthians 4:4 doesn't pull any punches about who is god of this place. Adam and Eve have given up their righteousness for an "apple," and God knows He will have to implement His plan of redemption if He is to ever again fellowship with the epitome of His creation. Man is the top of the pyramid of creation and was meant to be in fellowship with God forever. Because of Adam's sin, God has cursed the very earth on which Adam walked. I want to examine several verses that clearly spell out who has dominion in this world today. Then we will look at a real-world example that clarifies dominion versus sovereignty.

> And even if our gospel is veiled, it is veiled to those who are perishing. In whose case the god of this world hath blinded the minds of the unbelieving, so that they might not see the light of the gospel of the glory of Christ, who is the image of God. (2 Corinthians 4:3–4)

This verse gives an example of what Satan's strategic plan is here on earth. He wants to blind mankind's mind so that the glory of Christ cannot be seen. The glory of Christ is always present, but Satan tries to hide it. This gives credence to the idea of Satan having dominion over a domain of darkness. He has blinded men's minds, hence the darkness.

> And he, when He comes, will convict the world concerning sin, and righteousness, and judgment; concerning sin, because they do not believe in me; and concerning righteousness, because I go to the Father and you no longer see me; and concerning judgment, because the ruler of this world has been judged. (John 16:8–11)

So who is the boss here? What, or who, has God, in His sovereignty, allowed to be boss, the temporary ruler of this world? John 16:11 and 2 Corinthians 4:4 are verses that call him the "god of this world" and "the ruler of this world." Other verses verify and support those statements while saying it a different way. Let's look at the parable of the tares in Matthew 13:36–40 with a focus on verse 39.

> Then He left the crowds and went into the house. And His disciples came to Him and said, "Explain to us the parable of the tares of the field." And He said, "The one who sows the good seed is the Son of Man, and the field is the world; and as for the good seed, these are the sons of the kingdom; and the tares are the sons of the evil one; and the enemy who sowed them is the devil, and the harvest is the end of the age; and the reapers are angels. So just as

> the tares are gathered up and burned with fire, so shall it
> be at the end of the age." (Matthew 13:36–40 RSV)

Jesus is explaining the parable when he says in Matthew 13:39, "…
and the enemy who sowed them is the devil, and the harvest is the end of
the age; and the reapers are angels."

This parable can be seen as describing the ongoing battle on earth. The
battle is between good and evil, between God and the devil for the eternal
souls of men. The battle is between righteousness and unrighteousness.
Jesus is sowing the good seed of righteousness. The bad seed is being sown
by the devil.

In this parable, the devil is the one with power to sow unrighteousness
in the world. Unrighteousness is like a fatal health condition. It is a spiritual
condition that is terminal. Unrighteousness and sin go together and feed
off of each other. The outcome of sin is death. The wage of sin is death,
and that wage is always paid in full. Unrighteousness spreads from little
seeds in the mind to sinful acts in the flesh.

Righteousness, on the other hand, is like good health. It is not
contagious—it must be worked for and pursued. To grow and mature,
the seeds are sown and spread in the seedbed of your mind. The seeds
of righteousness require being inundated with the saving blood of Jesus,
coupled with large daily doses of His Word and regular consultation with
Jesus, the anointed one. The condition of righteousness exists exclusively
in the kingdom of God, and the seeds are looking for a place to grow.

I want to draw your attention to the fact that Satan has free reign on
earth to sow the seeds of sin. Even since Jesus's victory over him, Satan can
still lie, deceive, impersonate, kill, and steal. All he needs is for us to allow
him power. He has other tools in his toolbox, but he needs your permission
to use them as well. Once more, the battle is in your brain.

Ephesians 2 makes reference to the prince of the power of the air and
the spirit now working in the sons of disobedience. The "prince of the
power of the air" will become more significant as we get deeper into this
topic; it is simply another term for the devil. It is more descriptive of the
whole arena in which he is working.

As for you, you were dead in your transgressions and sins, in which you used to live when you followed the ways of this world and of the ruler of the kingdom of the air, the spirit who is now at work in those who are disobedient. (Ephesians 2:1–2 NIV)

Further support of Satan's position in this world is found in 1 John 5:19. John tells us about the sides involved in spiritual warfare. We who have chosen to become followers of Jesus Christ—especially we who have taken the next step from salvation to His lordship in our lives—have chosen our side. We have been redeemed. We have surrendered control to our Creator God by His grace given through His Son. He redeemed us. His Holy Spirit dwells in us. First John 5:19 describes our position on the battlefield clearly.

We know that we are of God, and that the whole world lies in the power of the evil one. (1 John 5:19)

Yes, "we know that we are of God." Is there a part of that verse we seem ignorant of? To me, the church of today doesn't seem to be clear about the fact that the world is not under our dominion. Even more troublesome is that this planet has not been redeemed. So where does the whole world lie?

First John tells us it is in the power of the evil one. It is abundantly clear why other scripture says we are to be *in* the world but not *of* this world. We are the aliens. This world is a place filled with fear, hate, sorrow, sickness, war, murder, rape, and any other hurtful antichrist activity or emotion one can imagine. Yes, we are aliens, but we are not powerless ghetto dwellers. The need to be separated becomes obvious. We need to be separated. We need to be in the world but not of the world.

Now judgment is upon this world; now the ruler of this world shall be cast out. (John 12:31)

Since the ruler of this world will be evicted, it is hard to assume that God is the ruler right now. This world is under judgment right now because of sin, Satan, and self. The S's are the problem, and Satan is the main one.

> I will not speak much more with you, for the ruler of the
> world is coming, and he has nothing in Me. (John 14:30)

We have another repetition of the ruler statement. Who is ruling this world now? Satan is. Only the Holy Spirit is holding him back. Paul affirmed this in 2 Thessalonians. God's Holy Spirit is currently restraining lawlessness.

> For the mystery of lawlessness is already at work; only he
> who now restrains will do so until he is taken out of the
> way. (2 Thessalonians 2:7)

This reign of grace will end. The Holy Spirit will be removed. Nothing will be holding back lawlessness. Will the Holy Spirit's absence be noticeable in the government? Will His absence be noticeable in the home or anywhere where people reside when He is taken out of the way?

> I do not ask that You will take them out of the world, but
> that You will keep and protect them from the evil one.
> (John 17:15 AMP)

The implication of this verse is in agreement with the 1 John verse quoted earlier. This verse is saying that, in this world, people are in danger and need protection from the evil one. Thank God He gave us that protection.

I have another Iowa farmer metaphor that illustrates what it is like for a follower of Jesus to be living in an evil environment. When vertical integration, or corporate farming, began to move into the area, huge livestock operations developed. First it was poultry, then pork, then dairy and beef. When thousands of any species of livestock are bunched together in one area, disease becomes a major threat. Over the years, there have been many responses to this problem.

Controlling the environment is one response. People who had a healthy facility went to great lengths to keep it healthy. One of the early responses to diseases in hog confinement buildings was a policy known as "shower in, shower out." Everyone who entered a confinement building, including laborers, bankers, owners, and hog buyers, had to take a shower going in and take a shower going out. No one was exempt from the rule because the idea was to keep the building as clean and free of health problems as possible. They did not want any germs moved from one facility to another.

Avoiding disease in a natural environment is similar to trying to avoid sin in the environment of this world. Exposure to sin has predictable results, just as exposure to disease germs has predictable results. Spiritual warfare is about identifying the issue correctly and making wise decisions. Peter put it another way.

> Beloved, I urge you as aliens and strangers to abstain from
> fleshly lusts, which wage war against the soul. (1 Peter 2:11)

Peter is saying that we must keep those things that will kill us out of our environment. I have heard believers say, "No fear here." If only we could add to that, "no unrighteousness here" or "no sin here." Peter tells us to stay away from those things that will cause you to lose the war against your soul.

Ultimately, the war is won or lost by decisions we make. It is about our choices. Satan will lie, but we are the ones who decide to believe it. Satan will accuse, but we have to accept the accusation. We have to validate the accusation for it to be of use to him. On the battlefield of spiritual warfare, we need to make right and righteous decisions. If we don't own whatever it is Satan throws at us, it is not ours.

Should we be surprised when we find ourselves in a hostile environment? No—we are righteous people living in a world that is under the temporary, somewhat limited power of the evil one. It is a world full of spiritual germs that we call sin. When we are in our Christian environment, we are (or should be) like the clean, disease-free environment that is so desirable to the livestock business. We ought to keep ourselves germ-free, or sin-free. When we leave the spiritual safety of our home, fellowship, the body of Christ, we are leaving the area where we thrive. When we go out into the world, we believers need the equivalent of a shower-in, shower-out program. We are entering a hostile place. We need to make sure we are getting under the umbrella of the blood of Christ. He will keep us safe and holy in spite of the evil we have to walk through. It could be called showering in and showering out with the blood of Jesus.

When I am in that unsafe world, am I going to try to be part of it? Am I going to fit in? Am I going to go along to get along? These questions determine that there is a choice to be made. It is a decision that will be made. The decision will be yes or no.

First Peter 1:2 points to the need for this precious blood of Jesus. He is talking about the sanctifying work of the Spirit. Jesus taught us to pray to our heavenly Father asking Him to protect us from evil. Father God's response was to give the Holy Spirit to whoever asks for it. He made available the mind of Christ, the name of Christ, along with lots of gifts and a book full of instructions.

> Peter, an apostle of Jesus Christ, to those who reside as aliens, scattered throughout Pontus, Galatia, Cappadocia, Asia, and Bithynia, who are chosen according to the foreknowledge of God the Father, by the sanctifying work of the Spirit, to obey Jesus Christ and be sprinkled with His blood: May grace and peace be yours in the fullest measure. (1 Peter 1:1–2 NASB)

When the Holy Spirit sanctifies something, it is complete. It is clean. It is germ-free. It is disease-free. It is set apart. It is holy, and it requires obedience.

That verse also says that we are to obey Jesus Christ. Faith is an action word, and we are told to be sprinkled with His blood.

In this portion of the study, we have been looking at the two sides in this battle that we are a part of. Luke's account of the temptation gives an interesting look at the devil's position.

> And he led Him up and showed Him all the kingdoms of the world in a moment of time. And the devil said to Him, "I will give You all this domain and its glory; for it has been handed over to me, and I give it to whomever I wish. Therefore if You worship before me, it shall all be Yours." (Luke 4:5–7)

In Luke's account of the temptation of Christ, the devil says he has been given domain or dominion over all the kingdoms of the world, and he can do with those kingdoms as he pleases. Jesus does not contest this claim. Jesus's response was to tell Satan not to tempt Him with that. Note in verse seven, Jesus tells him where to go and uses the Word to do it. In all the accounts of the temptation, Jesus seems to concede that the devil could give Him those things if he wanted. There is no statement that indicates that those things are not under Satan's dominion. So who is the boss right now? This conversation took place before the death and resurrection, so the enemy was at full strength. Jesus had not humiliated him yet.

The other verses we have looked at on this journey make it clear that the devil is still here, and he is still dangerous. He is still the temporary god of this planet. As nonbelievers, we are agreeing to live in his world of sin, death, and destruction until we agree to become a part of the kingdom of God. When we become ready and willing to proclaim that we are joint heirs with Jesus—when we have been filled with and empowered by the Holy Spirit—is when the devil loses all power over us. From that point on, he has only what we give him! That is when we become the aliens here.

Discussion Topics from Unit 5

According to 2 Corinthians 4:4, who is the temporary god of this world (implied)?

According to John 16:11, who is the ruler of this world?

According to 1 John 5:19, this world is under the power of whom?

According to Luke 4:5–6, what did Satan offer Jesus?

Why do you think Jesus did not contest Satan's right or ability to do what he offered?

Unit 6

Why Does God Allow This?

When people ask questions like, "Why does God allow things like that to happen?" or "Why do bad things happen to good people?" we can answer in the words of today. It is because of the "hood." In God's redemption plan, the neighborhood we are living in is owned by the worst slumlord in the universe, and we are just passing through. He is the one who will end up permanently evicted. When God the Father has completed His renewal project, our new neighborhood is going to have golden streets and will be lit by the glory of God. We are the aliens who need to learn to thrive while we are here.

Perhaps you were raised in an environment where you had to be street-smart to prosper, or even to stay alive. There are different rules of survival on different streets, aren't there? Sometimes being street-smart means simply knowing where the dangers are and learning how to avoid them. Sometimes it means knowing when the pizza place throws their stale pizzas in the dumpster so you can feed your kids today. Sometimes it means knowing when construction crews leave the homes they are working on and when they will return. If that knowledge is processed properly, you can provide free housing for yourself, family, or friends. It is about knowing the dangers and knowing how to achieve what you want in a hostile environment. Street smarts are specially learned skills.

Like the people in the tough neighborhoods of the inner cities, Christians have to be spiritually street-smart to survive and prosper. I am not talking about physically fighting but rather spiritually fighting. Christians are living in a hostile environment. They have to know the enemy. They need to know the rules and the tools that God has given them. The rules and the tools are the Word of God and His Holy Spirit. Christians need to learn the skills needed to thrive and survive. Those skills and that fight are what we call spiritual warfare."

This world we are visiting is evil. As we learn how to operate here, we will find ourselves enjoying more victories, both major and minor. Our testimonies will contain supernatural happenings.

It is generally accepted that Satan was "cut down to the earth" according to Isaiah 14:12, which we read at the start of this study. That biblical interpretation holds that one- third of the angels in heaven were in rebellion with Satan and were cast down with him. Revelation 12 makes reference to that one-third in verse 4. There are not many other Scriptures supporting this premise. In my understanding, Satan does not have the power to create. He can, however, pollute, confuse, convince, and deceive. He can lead mankind into perdition; he was capable of misleading angels he is still capable of misleading humans.

> Then another sign appeared in heaven: and behold, a great red dragon having seven heads and ten horns, and on his heads were seven diadems. And his tail swept away a third of the stars of heaven and threw them to the earth and the dragon stood before the woman who was about to give birth, so that when she gave birth he might devour her child. (Revelation 12:3–4)

Some say these fallen angels make up his hordes of demons. Others say they have become his evil spirits in addition to demons. All agree that he has legions of helpers. If Satan is unable to be in all places at all times, he has plenty of help. He has taught all of his help the rules he wants them to follow. They know the outcomes he wants. Neither Satan nor his crew is subject to the physical limitations that restrict us humans. We are talking about spirit beings here; they are real. They can manifest themselves in seemingly limitless ways and places. They are here to accuse, lie, kill, steal, and destroy just like their boss.

They can and will communicate with humans. Communicating with the spirit world is not endorsed in scripture. It happens a few times, but nowhere in scripture do I find instruction or modeling of conversing with anything other than people or angels. We are to exert control over all satanic beings. We should be prepared to tell them where to go and what to do in the name of Jesus. Don't allow yourself to get sucked into a discussion with the enemy.

Thus far in this study, we have systematically moved from the creation of man in God's image to a world that is evil. It has become a world with fallen man enjoying the moment. We have established that the devil has a mission and has the ability to implement the steps of his mission. He wants to separate mankind from God eternally.

We have established how he has gotten his power on earth and how prior to Jesus's appearance, man had little power in the spirit realm. Jesus's gift of victory has empowered man to be overcomers. After mankind's fall, God immediately began the process of redeeming the earth and mankind. With the passing of thousands of years, He sent the Redeemer who is the perfect sacrifice for sin. He won the battle with Satan. He has given us His Word and the presence of the Holy Spirit. The process of redemption will be completed following the return of Jesus. We who have decided to follow Jesus are the aliens here at this time.

Discussion Topics from Unit 6

According to Galatians 3:26–29, whose sons are we?

How did we get that position?

What happens when a person is "baptized into Christ"?

What does it mean to you when God says you are none of the things listed in verse 28, but "you are all one in Christ Jesus"?

According to Romans 8:15, what spirit have we not received?

Unit 7

Dominion vs. Sovereignty

Several times in this text, I have alluded to the confusion that sometimes accompanies the words "dominion" and "sovereignty." It is time to explain why the Bible can talk about the question of who is in charge and why we don't quite get it. Word definition can help clarify matters. Sometimes we just don't want to "get" it. It is easier to declare, "God is sovereign, and nothing happens if He doesn't allow it." Some years ago when I first began pondering what was happening when I heard Christians explain horrible happenings and use the words God is sovereign," I asked a pastor friend of mine about this theology that explained these things with the sovereignty of God. He replied, "I used to hide there."

Sovereign (noun): supreme ruler; (adjective): supreme in power

For clarification, we will use worldly examples of being sovereign. We think of nations as being sovereign, and to some extent they are. Even though we regard them as sovereign, they do not make good examples of the word. Since this world is imperfect, these examples will fall short of the completeness of God's sovereignty. I chose to use a series of anecdotes to demonstrate the difference between dominion and sovereign.

As a noun or an adjective, the dictionary definition fits our God, doesn't it? Yes, He is the supreme ruler, and yes, He does have supreme power in the universe. The only limitations on sovereignty are the ones the sovereign entity puts on Himself.

Most elementary-level Christians know that God is not going to send a world-ending flood; they know He won't do that because He promised He wouldn't. We know His Word is true and that He watches over it to perform it. We know He keeps the covenants He establishes.

That leads us to the concept of sovereign limitation. God made several covenants with His people. One of the very first things we established was that God gave dominion over the earth to His final creation, the cream of His crop, man and woman. God said they were to rule over the earth.

If the Lord gave man and (and He did) woman dominion over the earth, He wouldn't take it away. Some people quote Job 1:21, saying, "The Lord gives and the Lord takes away." I assure you that if God says it is yours, He will not ever take it away. If He would take it away after saying it was yours, that would make Him a liar. (However, don't be confused between ownership and stewardship. If God gives us stewardship over something, that is not the same as ownership, and it can be taken away.)

Many years ago, while working with Iowa State Extension's family program, I attended family mediation training of several days' duration. The instructor told the following story, which he represented as being true.

A mother and father had three grown children, all of whom were married. With the exception of one of their children, all was well with all four families. Mother and Dad were comfortably well off. Interpersonal relationships between the four families appeared to be healthy. The three children all had jobs and seemed to be doing nicely. The dilemma for the parents was that the home of one of the children had no refrigerator. Mom and Dad decided that the family should have a refrigerator; and being the kind of parents who believed in equity, their reasoning dictated that if one got a new fridge, then all three should get a new one. Since two of the families had excellent refrigerators, it didn't make sense to replace all of them. The parents also thought it might not be well accepted to buy one family a new item and give cash to the other two. In their eyes, the last reasonable alternative would be to investigate the price of a new appliance and give that amount of cash to all three families. That is exactly what they did. As the parents had hoped, all three of the grateful families spent the money on household improvements.

So if that was the case, what were they doing in a full-blown family mediation? The family without a refrigerator purchased the biggest home entertainment center they could get for the money. It was no longer a healthy extended family. Mom and Dad were furious. Everyone took sides. Relationships deteriorated until, in their natural eyes, mediation was the last hope. Before going any further with that story, let's define the word "dominion."

Dominion: (Noun)

As a noun, dominion is defined as, "The power or right of governing and controlling." The litmus test for the word "dominion" is: who has that final authority? Dominion must be transferred by or from the original entity that has both sovereignty and dominion.

Our American history books tell us that the Revolutionary War was fought over the right to self-government, dominion over their property. Because the colonists did not have that control, power, or dominion, many things were imposed on them in different areas of their life. In the beginning, people were hoping they would be able to stay under the sovereignty of England yet gain local control or dominion. They wanted the right to govern themselves while retaining the umbrella of a sovereign English nation.

Looking at the family story, who had sovereignty over all the money in the beginning? The parents did. Using those definitions, they had both sovereignty and dominion. The moment the money was in the hands of the children, Mom and Dad relinquished all rights to the money. Had they said, "We are giving you this amount of money, and here are the stipulations we are putting on it," they would have retained the power of control or dominion over it. But they were not supreme in power over the money they had given their kids. They had given up both sovereignty and dominion.

It doesn't take a rocket scientist to understand the point of that story. Even in the most basic human terms, when we give or transfer something to another, it is given without restriction. The person who receives a gift is free to do with it as he or she sees fit. The giving of a gift includes giving up the power or right of governing and controlling, whatever it is we are giving away. The recipient has dominion.

Remember the example of the accountability triangle? One side gave responsibility and tools, one side gave authority, and the third side had accountability. Giving a gift demands that the giver give both responsibility and authority as well as accountability over to the receiver.

The story of that family giving over dominion is a lot like what happens between God and His people. Adam and Eve were given Eden; it was for them. Responsibility and authority (dominion) were given with accountability.

God said, "I am going to make you rulers over all of this." God gave them the power or right of governing and controlling; He gave them free will with one very clear exception. He held them accountable. They chose to violate that trust. God's response was not to take back dominion. He had given it to them. He had given His Word and His gift. He did, however, choose to kick them out of the garden and curse the earth.

The parents in the refrigerator story had every right to disinherit the one family. They still had that much control. Mom and Dad just couldn't control how they spent what they had given away.

Man gave dominion to Satan when they chose to believe him rather than believe God. They sold out! They sold out for a reputed "apple."

The biblical account of the prodigal son also demonstrates this principle. When the son squandered his inheritance, it was gone. No one could stop it. It was a gift given with no conditions. When a gift is squandered, someone is going to be unhappy about it. In this case, it was not the father but the other son. The hardworking, stay-at-home, faithful, and obedient son was not overjoyed at his father's response to his brother's squandering.

This principle is important enough to spend time on one more example. Guantanamo Bay is a good example to help demonstrate the difference between dominion and sovereignty. It is universally known that the United States of America has a naval base on the island nation of Cuba, located at Guantanamo Bay. It is four hundred miles from Miami, Florida. It is the United States' oldest overseas naval base. It has been said to be a haven for iguanas and banana rats. Apparently it has an ideal climate and topography for them.

The United States leased this nearly three-million-acre plot of ground from Cuba near the end of 1903. A little more than thirty years later

(1934), the two nations agreed to continue the lease for a payment to Cuba of two thousand dollars in gold each year. Today that would be slightly more than an ounce of gold. They also agreed that the lease would continue to be in effect until both countries agreed to end it.

The United States and Cuba are sovereign nations. During the war on terrorism, following the attacks on the World Trade Center on September 11, 2001, the United States decided to keep POWs at Guantanamo Bay. Had Cuba disapproved of that practice, there would be no legal way for them to stop the United States from doing it. Yes, Cuba is a sovereign nation, and Guantanamo Bay is part of their nation. They, however, sold out their dominion over that place for a few dollars' worth of gold every year. Sounds familiar, doesn't it? Cuba sold out for gold rather than apples.

We have just looked at examples of the difference between sovereignty and dominion using examples from life in a family, examples of nations, and examples from the Bible. I hope that helps the reader to understand how the Creator God can, in His Word, refer to Satan as the "little g" god of this world.

We have looked in depth at the one side of this battle we call spiritual warfare. We have only looked at the losers. From the very beginning, God had a plan to restore mankind to a relationship with Himself. The plan was redemption through the blood of Jesus. God decided that He would give mankind one more chance to choose eternal fellowship with Him.

Much of the focus of Christianity, at least in the last couple of centuries, has been on salvation. Not overcoming, disciplining, or living a full and abundant life. Salvation became all about getting saved and then suffering through life until we get to heaven. Being saved has been allowed, in some circles, to become a static thing—as if salvation was the end rather than the beginning. We have seen generations of born-again Christians failing to live overcoming testimonies made possible by the blood of our Savior. We somehow have missed lordship. We can't be in God's army, "fighting the good fight," until we allow Jesus to be our commander in chief. That is His lordship.

> For you are all sons of God through faith in Christ Jesus. (Galatians 3:26–29)

Instead of being called "men" as in Genesis 1, Galatians now calls us "sons." It is a spiritual position—it means you belong to the family of God. It is a position unattainable by a person's own volition. It is not achievable by our own doing. No matter what gender a person is, they cannot attain the position of "son" without the blood of Jesus, without the grace of God! None of us can get there on our own. Praise the Lord that sonship through Christ is available to anyone. Male and female alike, it comes through grace.

What is the commonality here? What is the commonality between the "man" created in Genesis 1 and the "sons" in Galatians 3? These sons are a new creation, aren't they? What characteristic places us in this position of son? Righteousness!

Where did that new righteousness originate? How did the disobedient man attain enough righteousness to be called a son of God? He didn't and couldn't do anything. It was a gift given through grace and faith—a gift made possible by the death and resurrection of God's only begotten son. Praise the Lord. Being clothed in righteousness! How then do we possess this godly righteousness? Galatians 3:27 and Romans 13:14 tell us how.

> For all of you who were baptized into Christ have clothed yourselves with Christ. (Galatians 3:27)

Baptism by water? Baptism by fire? Baptism by the Spirit? Wise men can make much of those thoughts. I submit that if you honestly, as much as you are able, submit yourself to the lordship of Jesus, you will be led to the correct baptism. People who mean it when they say they are followers of Jesus Christ will be led to the baptism God wants them to have. Jesus said it better; He asked if we could drink of the same cup as He did. When people can and do honestly say yes to that question, they are walking under His lordship.

Be clear about who clothes us with Jesus. Sometimes we think all we have to do is to ask Jesus. The preceding verse and the following verse from Romans make it clear. You clothe yourself. You do it by accepting what He has done and by believing His Word. It says you have clothed yourself. He made it available; you have to put it on. Faith is an action word. One is to clothe himself in Jesus by faith. Romans 13:14 says, "But put on the Lord Jesus Christ, and make no provision for the flesh in regard to its lusts."

When we put on, or clothe ourselves with, Christ, we allow ourselves to be hidden in His righteousness. Why were the original men, that is, Adam and Eve, righteous? They were created that way. They were created in the image of the righteous God. They had not sinned; therefore, they were still righteous. When they made the decision to be disobedient and acted on it, they sinned. His righteousness was gone. There was only one rule or law to obey, and they chose to break it. They ate the apple. Sin abounded! When sin shows up, no one is righteous. Romans 3 explains.

> What then? Are we better than they? Not at all; for we have already charged that both Jews and Greeks are all under sin; as it is written, "There is none righteous, not even one." (Romans 3:9–10)

Why were we, who are mentioned in Galatians, called righteous? Because Jesus paid the perfect sacrifice to get us there. We must choose that position of righteousness just as Adam and Eve had to choose to abandon righteousness. Adam abandoned righteousness. Jesus Christ redeemed that gift—the opportunity to choose righteousness. Adam made a conscious decision to sin. He and Eve even talked about it before they made the decision. The problem is they talked about it with a serpent!

Jesus Christ, the Anointed One, made a quality decision to restore us. We became joint heirs of righteousness. We must make a quality decision that we want to receive God's restoring grace given through His Son. According to Galatians 3:27, we were baptized into Christ. At that time, we were clothed in righteousness. Jesus's death, resurrection, and ascension covered the nakedness God saw in the garden when man sinned! Jesus covered it with His own righteousness! He moved us from the curse of sin to the promise of life, of being heirs with Jesus, and of being eligible for the blessings (promises) available to Abraham.

> There is neither Jew nor Greek, there is neither slave nor free man, there is neither male nor female; for you are all one in Christ Jesus. And if you belong to Christ, then you are Abraham's descendants, heirs according to promise. (Galatians 3:28)

Discussion Topics from Unit 7

According to John 3:8, is spiritual activity easy to discern with natural senses? Why?

According to 2 Corinthians 10:4, our warfare weapons are not of what but are what and they will react by?

According to 2 Corinthians 10:5, are there things that exalt themselves against the knowledge of God?

What are those things called?

What should be done with them?

Unit 8

The Battleground

Second Corinthians 10 and Ephesians 6 tell where the battle is occurring. The battle is going on in the spiritual realm where it can't be seen. Outcomes of the unseen battles can be, and often are, seen in the physical realm. Outcomes are visible. Paul said they are evident. We are going to look at a few of them, but first we will see what John has to say.

> The wind blows where it wishes and you hear the sound of it, but do not know where it comes from and where it is going; so is everyone who is born of the Spirit. (John 3:8)

John 3:8 tells us that the Holy Spirit is like the wind; you can't see Him, but you can see what He does in the world. So it is in the spirit (with a small s) world. We can see the manifestation of the Holy Spirit—the outcomes of His work (if we are willing to see it), and we can see the manifestation of the demonic realm as well, if we are willing to acknowledge it. These outcomes are manifestations. The Bible lists manifestations that are not of God. We can come up with specific outcomes, many of which fall under headings already listed in the Bible. Galatians 5:17–21 lists some of the outcomes or manifestations as deeds of the flesh.

Today I would put addictions at the top of the list of fruits of the flesh. Everything on the list can be addictive. The current generation has witnessed huge increases in addictions of every imaginable kind. Perhaps in an outline for a freshman English class all of the addictions we have been trapped by would be under the heading of fruits of the flesh. Satan did not create these things. He cannot create. He can, however, pervert God's creations. When he perverts them, they come out the opposite of the holy creation. We can see the basis of spiritual warfare in Galatians.

> For the flesh sets its desire against the Spirit, and the Spirit against the flesh; for these are in opposition to one another, so that you may not do the things that you please. But if you are led by the Spirit, you are not under the Law. Now the deeds of the flesh are evident, which are: immorality, impurity, sensuality, idolatry, sorcery, enmities, strife, jealousy, outbursts of anger, disputes, dissensions, factions, envying, drunkenness, carousing, and things like these, of which I forewarn you, just as I have forewarned you that those who practice such things will not inherit the kingdom of God. (Galatians 5:17–21)

Notice the turnabout in this fruit. God created and ordains morality, purity, and sensitivity. Satan presents us with the options of immorality, sensuality, and impurity. God presents us with a living God, a risen Savior, and an indwelling Holy Spirit and life. Satan's substitutes are carnal idols made of earthly substances, demons that pervert, and death.

Having listed them as deeds of the flesh in those verses, Paul takes us right to the war in 2 Corinthians, chapter 10.

> I ask that when I am present I may not be bold with the confidence with which I propose to be courageous against some, who regard us as if we walked according to the flesh. For though we walk in the flesh, we do not war according to the flesh, for the weapons of our warfare are not of the flesh, but divinely powerful for the destruction of fortresses. We are destroying speculations and every lofty thing raised up against the knowledge of God, and we are taking every thought captive to the obedience of Christ. (2 Corinthians 10:2–5)

In verse 3, Paul distinguishes between walking according to the flesh, making war according to the flesh, and walking in the flesh. There are some connotations of the word "flesh" as it is used here. Flesh is used as the opposite of the Spirit. It is doing things in a manner not in agreement with God. In another usage, flesh also has a sense of visibility, the results of what is taking place in the flesh being visible to the natural eye. "We do not war according to the flesh," meaning that human, earthly wars are visible to the natural eye. The weapons used in spiritual warfare are not visible and often do not make sense in the natural realm. Destroying speculations, lofty things, and taking thoughts captive are not in any war strategy except God's.

We have developed the premise that these battles are fought in the mind. These verses support that premise and tell us how to respond. They use words like "destroy" and "take captive." Either word means to keep them under control or disable them. We decide if we will or if we will not accept as truth ungodly ideas of right and wrong.

"Lofty things" are human ideas like freedom of choice. In human terms, that is a lofty intellectual thing. To a dweller in the kingdom of God, it is debased and against the knowledge of God. We tend to view it as the one of the seven deadly sins that talks about the shedding of innocent blood. What are some other lofty things that can be raised up against the knowledge of God? Ungodly thoughts are unacceptable thoughts, and a quality decision must be made to respond to them. We can and should respond by quoting scripture back to those thoughts, by rebuking them in the name of Jesus, or by simply saying, "That is not my thought, and I am not going to accept it." There is a decision here. Thoughts that are in conflict with the Word of God need to be identified as foreign to who we are in Christ. Then we need to respond as who we are in Christ, using our authority and His Word. We should not accept these thoughts into our worldview as being okay because we think we live in a democracy or because Aunt Lucy believes that way.

Discussion Topics from Unit 8

According to Galatians 5:17, what are the two opposing forces in our walk?

Why does the flesh set itself against the Spirit?

According to Galatians 5:18, how does one get out from under the law?

According to Galatians 5:19, are the deeds of the flesh easy to see?

According to Galatians 5:21, what will those who practice those deeds *not* inherit?

Unit 9

The Battle of the Mind

Our battle is to bring down every deceptive fantasy and every imposing defense that men propose against the true knowledge of God. We even fight to capture every thought until it acknowledges the authority of Christ.

> … When they knew God, they glorified him not as God, neither were thankful; but became vain in their imaginations, and their foolish heart was darkened. (Romans 1:21 KJV)

Vain in this context means something along the lines of "no value." Vain thoughts or imaginations are without basis in fact. They have neither worldly validity nor spiritual fact. Vain imaginations are satanic twists to real-life happenings. If I am five minutes late getting home from a trip to the post office, my wife is thinking about who to get for pallbearers. That is a vain imagination. A father whose daughter is on her first date can have a lifetime of vain imaginations while she is having a milkshake at the local Dairy Queen. To fight the good fight, it is important to make a quality decision to not entertain those thoughts. You cast them down. You do it verbally, not just in your mind. Say to thoughts or imagination or speculation, "You are not of God, nor under the lordship of Jesus; get out of my mind and do not return." Cast them down. Use words.

Sometimes you might not be comfortable saying them aloud. If that is the case, say them very quietly. Satan and his imps may not be able to read your mind, but they hear really well when the name of Jesus is being used. Remember, we are warring in a realm where we cannot see the enemy, but we can see the results of his work. Those results will happen if we allow them.

Walking in the Spirit: a way of functioning that is in agreement with God's Word.

Walking in the flesh: a way of functioning that is the opposite of God's Word.

> For our struggle is not against flesh and blood, but against the rulers, against the powers, against the world forces of this darkness, against the spiritual forces of wickedness in the heavenly places. (Ephesians 6:12)

These spiritual forces are the forces that are able to put thoughts in your mind and convince you that acting on those thoughts will not be sin. This is exactly the same method Lucifer has been using since he got thrown out of heaven like a bolt of lightning. He puts a thought in one's mind that says, "That is not what God really said." or "That is not how he meant it." He seems to be able to imitate the still, small voice God often uses.

I have had this happen with things I have written. I once was involved in a dispute that needed resolution. This dispute was causing much trouble on a board of which I was a member. I compiled a written response, which I distributed in advance to the small group of people of interest in this matter. I wanted to state my position in writing so that it could not be misinterpreted. I carefully edited my document. During the meeting, one of the parties grossly misstated my premise. I responded that what he said was just the opposite of the printed copy in his hand. He argued back that what he had said was what I meant to say in my written presentation

Sometimes we rationalize being disobedient by convincing ourselves that we know what God meant—the opposite of what He says in His Word.

These forces with whom we war prefer darkness to light. These are forces that can and will bring wickedness to heavenly places. We need to decide: are we going to allow it or are we going to allow Jesus to be Lord in our lives?

Mark 16 tells about things in the world we are protected from if we are fulfilling His calling. Decisions to submit to Satan's dominion are another issue. Decisions to ingest substances that kill, steal, and destroy will ultimately do just that. Decisions that could have and should have been rejected when they were a thought will kill, steal, and destroy. The battle is not against flesh and blood! Flesh and blood are the spoils of the battle. Does Satan get the service of the physical body or does God? It is our decision.

> And the work of righteousness shall be peace; and the effect of righteousness quietness and assurance forever. (Isaiah 32:17 NIV)

One does not need to be a member of a satanic cult, be in a culture of addiction, or seek an experience with Satan in any other way. Satan is capable of interjecting himself any time he sees an opportunity. Interaction with him, be it intentional or unintentional, can have long-lasting negative effects in anyone's life and will totally disrupt the works of righteousness in our life. Peace will leave. Righteousness will leave. Quietness and assurance will be gone as well.

This next section is on "innocent" ways to get involved with the enemy of our soul. We need to guard the gates of our soul in order to keep the level of spiritual warfare as low as possible. By the way, what are these gates? I recently read in an article on automotive history that in the early days of automobiles, car doors were called gates. Gates are how we get in and out of things or places. If open, they allow access. If closed, they deny access. How do we give the enemy access to our soul? Just leave a gate open.

Briefly stated, those gates we need to keep closed are those that guard our natural senses. Satan will use anything that appeals to us through the senses. This becomes understandable if one thinks in terms that each of those natural senses must go to our brain to be processed. The spiritual war is started in the brain.

Nearly everyone has heard testimonies of instant addiction; usually the account is about meth. People tell about using only once, followed by a lifetime of recovery. Yes, "just a little bit" or "just one hit won't hurt" are lies from Satan, not global truths. He is very good at planting those thoughts in our mind. He can plant them with something we saw, smelled, tasted, heard, or touched. We sometimes seem to be very good at endorsing those thoughts and making them ours. We own them rather than resist them. They are just excuses using false logic rather than God's wisdom. We are prone to making ourselves easy targets for the enemy. It is often socially acceptable or even encouraged in our culture.

This subject of gates is purely spiritual and is initiated by the human, much to the delight of the enemy. Just as there are gateway drugs, there are many gateway activities that get us firmly aboard the losing side of the spiritual war. A loss in spiritual warfare occurs when anything becomes an idol—when anything is as important as God. I have known people who have made idols of their children, grandchildren, football, and automobiles. A person told me once that if dogs were not allowed in heaven, she did not want to go there. I am sure each and every one of those conditions could be explained away or justified by the person who possessed the idol.

The following scriptures don't seem to exempt using a divining rod for water witching, or holding a séance to ask Uncle Fred where he buried his money. Beware of the Ouija board, horoscopes, tarot cards, charms, and many other "innocent" games, including hypnotism. God's anointed leader of Israel found himself living a tormented life and a horrible death by messing with this innocent stuff. Saul was his name. The following verses contain the rules Saul did not want to acknowledge.

> Let no one be found among you … who practices divination or sorcery, interprets omens, engages in witchcraft, or casts spells, or who is a medium or spiritist or who consults the dead. Anyone who does these things is detestable to the Lord, and because of these detestable practices the Lord your God will drive out those nations before you. … The nations you will dispossess listen to those who practice sorcery or divination. But as for you, the Lord your God has not permitted you to do so. (Deuteronomy 18:10–12, 14 NIV)

Saul searched out a dead prophet to advise him, and it was downhill from then on. Verse 14 talks about that sin issue. It simply says, "Don't do it."

Discussion Topics from Unit 9

According to Ephesians 6:12, what is different about a spiritual struggle?

According to Ephesians 6:16, what is the function of the shield of faith?

According to Isaiah 32:17, what is the work of righteousness?

According to Ephesians 1:20, where is Jesus now?

According to Ephesians 1:22, what has been placed in subjection to Jesus?

Unit 10

The Struggle with Spirits

Galatians 5 introduces us to the New Testament instruction concerning the same issues discussed in unit 9.

> The acts of the sinful nature are obvious: sexual immorality, impurity and debauchery; idolatry and witchcraft; hatred, discord, jealousy, fits of rage, selfish ambition, dissensions, factions and envy; drunkenness, orgies, and the like. I warn you, as I did before, that those who live like this will not inherit the kingdom of God. (Galatians 5:19–21 NIV)

Again, we look at what happened to the Old Testament king, Saul. His decision cost him everything that was important to him. It cost his family, his health, and his kingdom; that is losing spiritual warfare. And it all resulted from acting on vain imaginations.

> What good is it for a man to gain the whole world, yet forfeit his soul? (Mark 8:36 NIV)

Spiritual warfare is about decisions. Mark 8:36 points out what the cost of some decisions can be. If Saul did not forfeit his soul, he must have come very close to it. God said He had taken His Holy Spirit from King Saul.

A comparison and contrast of King Saul and the Saul of the New Testament becomes interesting at this point: the Saul who ran into Jesus on the road to Damascus was vastly different from the king in the Old Testament. King Saul began his career chosen of God, anointed as king, revered as leader of a nation. He sinned, succumbed to the spirit of jealousy, of a spiritualist, and a lying spirit, to name a few. He ended life without hope, vainly trying to die the way he wanted. The Damascus road Saul started out as an elite religious fanatic who considered his calling to be the killing of God's people. He encountered Jesus on the road of life. He decided to follow God's will, in relationship with His Son, Jesus. He became a change agent for God. He, in the name of Jesus, demonstrated God's power through the Holy Spirit. He ended up on God's short list of what His people should be. He decided to follow Jesus. Spiritual warfare is about decisions.

Galatians is an awesome letter. It talks about being set free from Old Testament curses. It talks about being led by the Holy Spirit. Paul makes it clear, though, that what was said in Deuteronomy 18 is still in effect. We don't do witchcraft, sorcery, or divination. First, if we do make contact with the spirit world, it will be with evil spirits. Secondly, if we make contact, we are in conflict with God's Word, which is a sin.

The company for which I worked had more than two hundred employees. They hired a hypnotist for entertainment at their semiannual agency meeting, at which attendance was mandatory. I refused to attend and was the only one in the agency to refuse. I followed company protocol by contacting my supervisor, who also happened to be the executive director of the agency. In a gentle voice, I told her it would be a violation of my beliefs to attend. Since she had been exposed to my testimony over the years, she agreed that I should not have to go to that part of the meeting. The buzz after the meeting was about one of my staff members who volunteered to be part of the show. Comments centered on how out of character her behavior was when she was hypnotized. She had given up control of her mind and her value system. That is not a position a child of God wants to be in. One Christian came to me later and told me that he wished he had gotten an exemption as well.

In Galatians 5, God prohibited us from initiating contact with the spirit world. It falls under witchcraft. Therefore, His angels obey God's laws and do not respond to attempts by us to make direct contact. If we attempt to make any contact with the spirit world, evil spirits will take advantage of this sin and contact us, claiming to be good. God does send angels to us more than we realize. Sometimes it is in response to our prayers, but they normally do not make direct visible or verbal contact. Demonic spirits will respond to human efforts to contact the spirit world. There are fantastic accounts in the Bible of angelic activity in a body or on earth. They just aren't the norm. We are to be in continual contact with God. Pray and listen. What does God want us to be doing?

In the early spring of 1957, as a member in good standing with the US Army, I was given a free ocean cruise across the North Atlantic. We departed from Brooklyn Naval Yard and landed at Bremerhaven, Germany. We left the moorings from Brooklyn late in the afternoon. During the time we were in the harbor, the ship slowly and gently rolled, making one think that crossing the ocean in a ship would be a pleasant trip. Sometime after darkness on our first night out, the ship stopped for a brief period. Since we had no view to the outside, one could only wonder what was happening. Why did we stop? Certainly none of us army boys who were in the troop compartment just above where nonhuman stuff (cargo) was carried knew what was going on.

Ten to fourteen days later, we were close to seeing the coast of Germany. This time when the ship stopped, it was daylight. We were standing on the deck and saw a small craft approaching. Our ship stopped, the small craft pulled up beside us, and a man came onboard our ship. A harbor pilot was coming on board.

I learned that the personnel on an ocean vessel are not allowed to sail into a harbor without this special person to guide them. Because of the special skills he or she has, this person is given the authority to bring the ship into the harbor and land it at the appropriate dock. This authority is given to them by the higher authority of the nation whose harbor they are entering. The captain of the ship has the authority to sail the open seas but not to enter harbors.

Is that delegated authority by itself enough to qualify one to take a ship into a harbor? No? Why not? That harbor pilot has to learn all of the rules and protocols that are specific to that harbor. He or she has to prove that knowledge and skill before the authority is given.

That person needs to know the currents, the winds, the hidden obstacles, along with anything else that could cause the ship to sink or cause damage to another ship. The authority by itself without the training does not qualify a person for the job.

We are entering another phase in training for the battle. We are going to be looking at a transfer of authority and training in the hazards we might encounter. Different harbors have different threats. None of us desire to become the spiritual version of the *Titanic*. That ship hit a mostly submerged piece of ice, in the dark of the night in the fog. That is not the fate God wants for His warriors.

While doing research for some family history, my brother ran into an account of a man from a farm that joined ours. His name was Bill Duff. Bill was drafted into the Iowa militia during the Civil War. Two weeks later, he was at a battle in Nashville, Tennessee, just two weeks from inscription to battle. We scoff at that because we know a person who is in the service for only two weeks is not prepared for combat. Unfortunately, we Christians tend to send new recruits into the battle without adequate training. Just like Bill Duff, they are told to always be courageous. We give them a verse or two from Joshua, telling them to "go fight the good fight," and head them out the door. We just let them wander into the world. Like Bill Duff, they often get seriously injured. Bill did survive the battle. Later in the Civil War, he was seriously wounded but survived the wound. After the war, he came back to the farm, where one of his own bulls killed him in his own barnyard. My brother suggested that he probably was not known as "Lucky Willie."

Like Bill Duff, each of our battles will require a little different skill to survive unscathed. That bull presented a completely different set of threats than the Confederate Army had presented. The good news is that God already knows what the threats of spiritual warfare are, and He has written a manual to teach us His strategies. I had an instructor in college who, upon passing out an exam, would walk to the chalkboard. There, in huge bold letters, he would write, "Read the dang questions." It is that simple for us too. We have to read the instructions.

We were discussing gates in a previous unit. All gates should be open to the Word of God and teaching from His Word. Following the instructions after reading them is a good idea as well. For the Christian, there is training that will teach a person to land safely in the correct harbor. It will be a harbor safe from the stormy seas of life. Those storms will come, but they will not destroy us. God calls it equipping the saints.

We are all learning to identify hazards. Many of those hazards are hard to recognize if they aren't above water. If they aren't properly identified, they cannot be easily avoided. It is wise to read through a few scriptures, many of which are familiar, to see if we can apply them to our spiritual battles.

> But seek ye first his kingdom, and his righteousness; and all these things shall be added unto you. (Matthew 6:33 KJV)

Why should we seek His kingdom? Why should we seek His righteousness? Why are those things in God's great war manual? If your answer is so that "all these things shall be added unto you," you might be on the wrong trail. If one is seeking the kingdom and righteousness for the reward of all these things, he has the wrong motivation. But if you are doing these things because you want to be obedient to God, you are closer to a workable answer. Obedience will be rewarded.

> And do not be conformed to this world, but be transformed by the renewing of your mind, so that you may prove what the will of God is. For through the grace given me, I say to every one among you not to think more highly of himself than he ought to think: but to think so as to have sound judgment, as God has allotted to each a measure of faith. (Romans 12:2–3)

Why shouldn't we be "conformed to this world"? I recently heard a person say that if you think everything is as it ought to be in this world, you just aren't paying attention. That may be the simplest answer to why we need to let God fashion us to His liking.

When civilians go into the military, what is the first thing that must happen to them? They must be transformed. Their appearance is transformed. Their hair is cut. They are issued identical uniforms. Most of them are taught a new way of thinking and problem solving. They learn how the enemy presents himself as well. These changes are what Bill Duff, the Civil War soldier, didn't get. I knew a pastor and his wife whose son had just completed his first eight weeks of military training. His parents went to his graduation. At the end of the ceremony, the graduates were left in formation, and the parents were to come down from the stands and find their soldier. The pastor and his wife took three tries to find their son; he had been transformed.

When we become Christians, we are given the choice of being transformed. Some are so radically changed that even parents don't recognize the language and the new way of thinking that their children are using. This person is now in God's army. When God has finished this initial transformation, the world should see the difference. The heathen should see it and either rage at us or want to join us.

God is sovereign. If he truly had dominion over this world right now, we would not be worrying about the how, why, and when of spiritual warfare.

I want to nail down the content of some verses we examined earlier in this study. They are critical to understanding the essence of those who, why, what, and where questions of each of our personal battles with the enemy. There will also be corporate battles we engage in because we belong to the body of Christ. I think some of the misconceptions we have about spiritual warfare come from well-intended teaching about the sovereignty of God. Yes, God is the Creator of the universe. He is just, honest, and won't lie. I would encourage the reader to review the questions at the end each previous section. A review of those questions will help with clarification on this topic. Yes, this planet is in God's universe. He has ordered the universe, and all creation is ordered by Him. How could it be that He does not have total dominion over planet Earth?

We have clearly established that God gave dominion over planet Earth to Adam and Eve. In Genesis 3, they chose to follow Satan's words rather than God's words. In doing that, they sold themselves. They sold the dominion over themselves to Satan. They had a choice.

Today we have a choice, a choice just as they had. Joshua in the Old Testament said he and his house were going to serve the Lord. He made a choice. We cannot redeem the world! Nor can the world redeem us. Adam and Eve made a choice that resulted in a life in the kingdom of darkness.

Jesus came so that we can have the choice to begin living in the kingdom of light rather than the kingdom of darkness. God so loved the world? He loved it so much He died for it! How can that be?

Neither the devil nor man can control the earth's orbit, tides, sunrise, and sunset. God is the only one who can do that. He is implementing His plan of redemption on His timetable. We are in the here and now and would do well to get equipped for the here and now. We are still physically in an evil place, spreading the Word while we wait. That seems to irritate the enemy.

God told us to not be conformed to this world. Why did He give us this instruction in Romans 12? God told us this because we are called to be holy. Satan, the ruler of this world, is evil, the opposite of holy. Satan is the one who leads humans to sin, and the wage of sin is death. He is the caretaker and distributer of darkness. Given access, he would bring darkness into every human life. Jesus is the provider of light that leads to holiness. According to John 10:10, Jesus is the one who leads us to a full and abundant eternal life. We must conform to Him rather than this world. We truly should endeavor to be like Jesus.

Yes, we are aliens, but we are powerful aliens, just as Jesus was. He was all human while He walked this earth. He was also fully God. We have power and authority, just as He did. We are in the process of discovering those powers. We are in the process of being transformed into redeemed, holy, set-apart warriors. We are warriors in God's earthly army with the mind of Jesus available to us.

> When you were dead through your transgressions and the uncircumcision of your flesh, He made you alive together with him, having forgiven us all our transgressions; having canceled out the certificate of debt consisting of decrees against us, which was hostile to us; and he has taken it out of the way, having nailed it to the cross; when He had disarmed the rulers and authorities, He made a public display of them, having triumphed over them through Him. (Colossians 2:13–15)

All of the supernatural happenings listed in those three Colossians verses were the direct result of the death of Jesus at the cross. Grace truly abounded at the cross. Verse 13 says we were dead in our carnal fleshly sin. Then it says because of Christ's death God brought us to life. He brought us to eternal life. What grace!

Verse 14 puts it in legal terms and reads like a court document. Although we were known to be guilty of all charges, they were dropped. There is no record of what we did. All of that was nailed to the cross, and from there it disappeared. Praise the Lord.

Verse 15 explains one more spiritual happening at the cross. That happening was the disempowerment of Satan that was detailed earlier. All of that was at the cross.

We looked at these verses early in this study. We are at the point now where we can take a more in-depth look at how this impacts us today. In Genesis 3:15–16, God cursed Satan. According to this Colossians verse, Jesus, at the cross, defeated and humiliated him. Jesus disarmed rulers and authorities. Those victories were over the ruler of this world, Satan. That defeat took away his power, but he is still referred to as the temporary ruler of, or god of, this world. So right now, we are aliens in a world whose god has been empowered to fail, whose god has been defeated and humiliated, and whose god has been destined to the lake of fire. How does this compare to "having been given eternal life and having it abundantly"?

God was not finished. He had more to do and another place to do it. He tells us about it in Ephesians, chapter one. Ephesians 1 tells about the embellishment or totality of the empty tomb.

> … Which He brought about in Christ, when He raised Him from the dead and seated Him at His right hand in the heavenly places, far above all rule and authority and power and dominion, and every name that is named, not only in this age but also in the one to come. And He put all things in subjection under His feet, and gave Him as head over all things to the church. (Ephesians 1:20–22)

According to the Colossians verses, when sin was nailed to the cross, Jesus disarmed and defeated the enemy. Christ then received a position above all other positions in the universe. Not just above but far above. It clearly states this happened when God raised Jesus from the dead. Satan, at the moment of the resurrection, lost all of the things he bragged about getting in the Isaiah scriptures, which we toured at the beginning. He also lost the power of sin and death. Death no longer had any sting. What was placed in subjection to Jesus? All things.

According to these verses, how long will all things be in subjection to Him? Starting now and lasting forever. The empty tomb completed His work. He ended up where Satan said he wanted to be. Jesus's victory over death gained Him the highest, most powerful position in all of creation.

When I was a little boy, baseball was still the sport of the nation. Whenever a few boys gathered together, a few gloves would show up along with a baseball bat and a baseball. We would choose sides, and everyone knew who the first four players chosen would be. They were the best.

In this battle we are in, I am so thankful I can be on Jesus's team. He is the winner. He equips us, and He sends us where He has gone.

Discussion Topics from Unit 10

According to 1 Peter 2:11, what did Peter call followers of Jesus?

What does that verse tell us to leave alone?

Why should we leave them alone?

According to Romans 12:2, how should we be changing?

According to Colossians 2:13, how many of our transgressions are forgiven?

Unit 11

Jesus's Expeditionary Force

> Now after this the Lord appointed seventy others, and
> sent them in pairs ahead of Him to every city and place
> where He Himself was going to come. And He was saying
> to them, "The harvest is plentiful, but the laborers are
> few; therefore beseech the Lord of the harvest to send out
> laborers into His harvest." (Luke 10:1–2)

In these two verses, Jesus commissions His followers. He gives them
direction and a reason to accept the commission. These and the verses
following are part of the process of transferring authority.

Jesus sent His followers to the place where He was going to appear. He
empowered them so He would be recognized as the source of the power
the group had been operating in. He would need no introduction when he
traveled this route. Remember the accountability triangle? He gave them
the task and responsibility. He gave them the authority and tools needed
to perform the task. The third side of the triangle was reporting back to
Him (accountability).

> Go; behold, I send you out as lambs in the midst of wolves.
> Carry no money belt, no bag, and no shoes; and greet no
> one on the way. (Luke 10:3)

For those who were sent, the success of the venture required a reliance
on His Word for their daily needs to be met. They had to believe what

He said was truth. That is faith in operation. Faith is a verb; it is an action word. Their action was to implement this plan not by taking but by receiving. Like a well-run mission that relies on God for their very existence, they were to demand or require nothing but were to receive everything. What a difference in mind-set.

> Whatever house you enter, first say, "Peace be to this house." If a man of peace is there, your peace will rest on him; but if not, it will return to you. (Luke 10:5)

Jesus tells them that peace is to be their currency. It is a currency that is only good to those who choose to receive it. There is no room for pride to operate in this system. Like Paul, we must brag only about the Lord. Like Peter and John, we have to say, "What we have, we will give unto you." In this part of the kingdom of God, peace is the currency, and pride is a currency of no value.

When we decide to follow Jesus, we are choosing to leave the kingdom of darkness. We must be able to do it in the spirit of these two verses. We must be able to say to everyone in the world, "I offer you what I have received." At the beginning of Luke 10, Jesus told the seventy the harvest was ready, meaning there were many people ready to follow Him, to become what we now call Christians. If that is not acceptable to a person, or a group of people, we must move to where people are willing to hear the message of Jesus. That is where the harvest is.

When we are in the kingdom of darkness, we operate by what we can see. When we are operating in God's kingdom of light, we operate by what we can't see. What a paradox that is! Second Corinthians 5:7 calls it walking by faith, not by sight.

> Stay in that house, eating and drinking what they give you; for the laborer is worthy of his wages. Do not keep moving from house to house. Whatever city you enter and they receive you, eat what is set before you. (Luke 10:7)

I think these two verses address what I call modern and historic misapplication of missionary work and evangelism. That sin, if I can be so bold as to identify something as sin, is to demand that a new believer do as I do. You must eat this because this is what I eat. You must do everything that I do, and do it the way I do. It is saying, "You must be like me, or I will not accept you." That is evangelizing culture, not Christ! That group of followers was sent out with the instructions, "If they accept you, you accept them."

> … And heal those in it who are sick, and say to them,
> "The kingdom of God has come near to you." (Luke 10:9)

When those criteria are met, the sick are healed and the kingdom of God is there. When we are where God wants us to be and have a heart like God's, the Holy Spirit will be working through us to the glory of His grace. Like those seventy, we can say, "One greater than us is coming soon."

Now comes the bad news: those who refuse to hear the good news had better be prepared to hear the bad news.

> But whatever city you enter and they do not receive you,
> go out into its streets and say, "Even the dust of your city
> which clings to our feet we wipe off in protest against you;
> yet be sure of this, that the kingdom of God has come
> near." (Luke 10:10)

The bad news starts out with God's "agents" (by that I mean the people God has commissioned to spread the good news) giving up on you. Those agents are instructed to leave because the kingdom of God has come near to you and you have refused to receive it. God's agents were sent out where Jesus was planning to go in the near future. Jesus simply told them to go where they were accepted. In the following verses, he compared those places of rejection to other cities famous for not accepting the Word.

> I say to you, it will be more tolerable in that day for
> Sodom, than for that city. (Luke 10:12)

Things are not looking good for a city that is told that Sodom had an easier go of it than they will have if they refuse to accept the good news.

Sodom, after all, was destroyed by fire and brimstone in response to God's wrath.

> "Woe to you, Chorazin! Woe to you, Bethsaida! For if the miracles had been performed in Tyre and Sidon which occurred in you, they would have repented long ago, sitting in sackcloth and ashes. But it will be more tolerable for Tyre and Sidon in the judgment than for you. And you, Capernaum, will not be exalted to heaven, will you? You will be brought down to Hades! The one who listens to you listens to Me, and the one who rejects you rejects Me; and he who rejects Me rejects the One who sent Me." (Luke 10:13–16)

After Jesus is proclaimed and the signs and wonders have been performed, it is time for people to make a decision. If Jesus is not then received by the people, it becomes time to preach hell, fire, and damnation as Jonah did or as John the Baptist preached. Jesus is comparing the cities where He has been in the flesh—cities of His time—to the infamous cities of the past. He tells the cities of His time that the cities of the past, as sinful as they were, would have repented had they been exposed to Him, to His works, and to His teaching.

> The seventy returned with joy, saying, "Lord, even the demons are subject to us in Your name." And He said to them, "I was watching Satan fall from heaven like lightning. Behold, I have given you authority to tread on serpents and scorpions, and over all the power of the enemy, and nothing will injure you. Nevertheless, do not rejoice in this, that the spirits are subject to you, but rejoice that your names are recorded in heaven." At that very time, He rejoiced greatly in the Holy Spirit, and said, "I praise You, O Father, Lord of heaven and earth, that You have hidden these things from the wise and intelligent and have revealed them to infants. Yes, Father, for this way was well-pleasing in Your sight." (Luke 10:17–21)

Jesus's expeditionary force of seventy people came back excited. Numbers 13 is an account of another small expeditionary action. Many years before Jesus sent the seventy, God had Moses send out twelve people from the leaders of the tribes of Israel. They were to explore the Promised Land that the tribes were approaching. They scouted out the land to which God had brought them. They came back with a negative and frightened majority. Ten of the twelve said they should not even try to possess what God had promised them. Two were excited at the prospect of seeing how God would do this miracle through His people. The result of the decision not to follow God's leading? Forty years in the wilderness and the death of every adult who made that decision. God did not look favorably on people who refused His grace at the time of Moses, and the previous verses from the book of Luke tell us He still does not look favorably on disobedience.

The seventy who went out on an expedition in obedience to Jesus came back excited. It was not the kind of excitement that comes from attending a Holy Spirit conference or being a part of a fifty-thousand-person evangelical meeting in an outdoor stadium with great praise and worship time. They had discovered the reality of Jesus. They discovered who He was, His relationship with them, and His position in the universe. They made this discovery working one on one with people to whom Jesus had sent them. They came back so caught up in the work they had been assigned that Jesus felt the need to calm them a little. He slowed them by pointing out what should really excite them. With that said, one must point out that by verse 21, Jesus is exuberant as well.

Just as the devil said, "It is mine and I can give it to you" at the time of the temptation in Luke 4:6, Jesus was saying to the seventy, "The authority to do these works is mine and I am giving it to those who believe." He said it, and he demonstrated it!

In this account, Jesus is exercising His authority even before the cross, even before the empty tomb. In verse 19, He delegates His authority to a group of humans—people like us. What happened in verse 17? Even the demons displayed their subjection. To what were they subject? The name of Jesus. "In the name of Jesus" is not just something we say before we say, "Amen!" It is the most powerful phrase in the universe.

Verses 20 and 21 tie it all together. What has happened has happened because verses 17, 18, and 21 reflect the joy of walking in the spirit of faith (even though the word faith is not used). Verse 21 tells us He is talking about faith by using the word "infant." Faith of a child is what we are supposed to have, and then we will have eyes to see! We are warned to see this from the greater perspective of victory over sin and death for eternity, as well as victory over a defeated enemy in the immediate world.

I am concerned that today's Christianity seems to celebrate neither of these victories. Not wanting to see anything in Jesus's victory over sin and death is a horrible betrayal of mankind. Saying nothing of the other fantastic works that Jesus is still doing is wrong as well. He is still, through His Holy Spirit, healing, offering deliverance, and making peace. His victory in our immediate lives is important. In the opening of this study, I stated a concern about how the heathen sees us and how we see ourselves. When we began to live in His victory, it will be noticed by all. There are still those who recognize and preach Jesus as Savior. Praise God for them— thank God for the souls they are introducing to Jesus. Many of those who are not being told what God is still doing are missing the experience of Jesus in the now. The name of Jesus Christ is the key to victory. Jesus said it in another way in Mark.

> Truly I say to you, whoever does not receive the kingdom
> of God like a child will not enter it at all. (Mark 10:15)

In the verse above, Jesus is talking about a mind-set. Children learn to trust their parents. They know with certainty they will be fed and cared for by their earthly parent. Receiving the kingdom like a child requires trust. To act like a child in receiving the kingdom of God requires trust because it requires a relationship. The kind of faith that seems childlike causes one not only to believe but to act as well.

Two of our granddaughters grew up in a southeastern Minnesota community of several thousand people. This community demonstrates values of an earlier era. They recognized the integrity of the parent. Beginning at an early age, perhaps five or six, their mother could send either of them to the hardware store, grocery store, or pizza place with instructions to get an item and "charge it." Those businesses knew their parents had those kids' backs and treated them as they would have treated the parent.

Satan has the same response when God's children use the name of Jesus. Satan becomes compliant. He knows who has God's kid's back.

Correctly using the name of Jesus is the key to success in spiritual warfare. The name of Jesus is to be used by a person who is not ashamed to cry out, "in the name of Jesus." Whenever there is a need for it. His name is for those who use it simply because it works.

A baby quickly learns that crying will prompt an action, be it feeding or fixing. Crying out in the name of Jesus results in a solution to the problem. It requires trust that comes from God through His grace. Once again, there is a possession issue for the believer. God told Moses that He was going to take all His people to the Promised Land. There was a catch, wasn't there? They had to possess it.

How do I possess the kingdom of God? We start by believing Jesus is who He says He is and accepting what He has made available to us. I can do it by believing His Word without exception, by receiving God's Son as Savior, and inviting His Holy Spirit to dwell in and empower me and to equip me. Possession of God's promises always involves His faith imputed in you. As I've stated before, faith is an action word. From the beginning of Jesus's earthly ministry, He has chosen common people to be His people. Then He gifts them to accomplish His mission.

Discussion Topics from Unit 11

According to Luke 10:1, who was going to tour the same places where the seventy were sent?

According to Luke 10:4, what were the seventy not to take with them?

According to Luke 10:8, what were they to eat?

According to Luke 10:9, what were they to do?

According to Luke 10:17, who gave them power and authority to do the assigned task(s)?

Unit 12

There Is a Spirit World

We need to examine some of the spirits mentioned in Bible. Some of them are God-given to help us in this life. Others, the unholy spirit beings, are a part of Satan's forces and are here to kill, steal, and destroy. We will find out in more detail who the battle is with and what that discovery means.

I am going to start with a scriptural overview of spirits empowered by God to help His people in an alien environment. The spirits we will be examining first are God-given spirits.

A word search of the whole Bible revealed some six hundred passages containing the word "spirit" with either a capital S or lowercase s. Generally speaking, the capital S Spirit references God's Holy Spirit. The lowercase word spirit references the spirit of man. This is the spirit that, since the fall of man, has been referred to as the spirit of man or woman.

There is nothing holy about a spirit until it has surrendered to the Spirit of God. The last group of spirits mentioned in scripture is satanic and demonic. They are the ones against whom we find ourselves fighting our daily battles. They don't go away until they are told. Their influence begins in our mind as they try to influence our thinking, which then influences our actions, which then influences our spiritual, intellectual, and physical well-being.

The tri-division list of types of spirits described above is not an exhaustive list of references. I have tried to make it a representative list. Each one will be introduced by a specific scripture reference followed by a commentary.

Then the LORD said, "My Spirit shall not strive with man
forever, because he also is flesh; nevertheless his days shall
be one hundred and twenty years." (Genesis 6:3)

When Genesis says "my Spirit," it is clear that this is God speaking.
He is speaking of His Holy Spirit, a full partner in the Trinity of God. He
was an action agent in creation, and He is now the action agent in our lives
and in our world (that is, if we allow it). Thank God, He sent His Spirit to
us after Christ's ascension to the Father.

Notice the address on this verse. Genesis 3:6 takes place after the
fall. God identifies His Holy Spirit and makes it clear that His Spirit is
still striving with man, but that is not how it is always going to be. Man,
who was created in God's image, has chosen to be flesh. This verse uses
the phrase, "he [man] also is flesh." Man is a spirit, with a soul and a
body. He has chosen disobedience over obedience. He chose darkness over
light. Then God stamped him with an expiration date, much the same as
perishable food products in grocery stores are labeled with "use before"
dates.

He created us to walk with Him forever in righteousness. After
unrighteousness became a part of us, our shelf life shrunk to 120 years.
Obviously most humans haven't been making it that far. Living in an
evil world that has surrendered to sin has taken its toll on our longevity.
Genesis 7 tells us more about man and the spirit realm.

… Of all that was on the dry land, all in whose nostrils
was the breath of the spirit of life, died. (Genesis 7:22)

Just a few chapters earlier in Genesis 2:7, God breathed life into man.
There is now a spirit of life. That spirit is no longer eternally, automatically
sustaining man with God. This is the spirit of life as it exists in the flesh,
or in carnal man. This spirit is not evil. It does respond to the Word of
God and the name of Jesus. Just as our Bible indicates, all of creation will
respond. In context, this is talking about man's spirit after man had chosen
to walk in the flesh. This spirit is eternal but not guaranteed an eternity
with the Father.

> You shall speak to all the skillful persons whom I have endowed with the spirit of wisdom, that they make Aaron's garments to consecrate him, that he may minister as priest to Me. (Exodus 28:3)

Many people have skills or talents that are uniquely theirs. A skill set or a talent is a gift that can and should be honed and polished by training, by practicing the way Olympic athletes do. We are to do all things as if we are doing them for the Lord. Interestingly, God considers His gifts to us as being irrevocable.

In the verse above, God is telling Moses there are some whom He has endowed with a spirit of wisdom. This seems to be a more job-specific wisdom than the wisdom listed in 1 Corinthians 12:8. Exodus craftsmen are accompanied by a spirit of wisdom to guide them in the use of their God-ordained talent or skills.

Some Christian fellowships use a "tool" they have developed to help identify the gifting of the individuals in their group. The tool or test is based on the many spiritual gifts detailed in the New Testament.

I was discussing this practice of testing with a Bible teacher whom I respect highly. He suggested that if the leadership of a church doesn't recognize the gifting of the congregation for whom they are responsible, perhaps the leadership isn't holding the position in the body of Christ that God intended for them.

Many individual believers struggle when they feel they are not competent enough to contribute to the body of Christ or to honor God. Sometimes they do know the areas where God wants to use them or has gifted them. That situation can become frustrating, and a frustrated individual is vulnerable to a divisive spirit. The divisive spirit is an evil spirit, and I mention it here in passing. For now, it is enough to say it does exactly what the name implies.

When the divisive one is on the scene, spiritual warfare manifestations will soon show up. Blaming starts because no one involved knows how to fight a battle with unseen forces. Sometimes an individual believes the lie that they have nothing to offer. Other times, an individual might think of himself more highly than he ought, which is also lying to oneself.

Who is the father of lies? Satan and his evil spirits are lying specialists. Old Lucifer is the father of lies. He was a failure as a snake, and he is a failure as a toothless lion with no claws. He was defeated at the empty cross. He was humiliated at the empty tomb. He is trying to have a negative impact on the holy body of Christ, and he can only do it if we allow it. This is an example of the essence of spiritual warfare. It starts in the mind, and each battle is won or lost in the mind. Satan does not have control of your mind. He will never have control of your mind if you don't give it to him. The spirit of wisdom helps move our God-given skills and talents from the realm of natural to the realm of the supernatural.

> … That the God of our Lord Jesus Christ, the Father of glory, may give to you a spirit of wisdom and of revelation in the knowledge of Him. (Ephesians 1:17)

Once again, this time in the New Testament, this spirit of wisdom shows up—along with revelation and knowledge. Sometimes these spirits are referred to almost if they were conjoined twins or triplets. They go together. There can be no wisdom of value if that wisdom is separated from knowledge of God.

Solomon asked God for wisdom to rule God's people when God offered him anything he wanted. Paul is telling the people of Ephesus that he is praying that they might have the same God-given wisdom, along with revelation and knowledge of God's will. We have every scriptural right to ask God for the same things.

We should be able to ask for this with expectancy. The expectancy comes not because we deserve anything; it comes because of God's abundant and bountiful grace. He has given all of us a measure of faith, and expectancy is a manifestation of faith. Expectancy can also be a matter of experience. When God has allowed us the privilege of seeing His response to His people when they pray according to His Word, we will pray with expectancy. We will not only expect it but we will get excited about it.

Spirit of holiness

… Who was declared the Son of God with power by the resurrection from the dead, according to the Spirit of holiness, Jesus Christ our Lord. (Romans 1:4)

The attribute of holiness is so important to God. He, in His divine understanding, knew that we were going to need a lot of help to understand it. I view all of the spirits of God as aids to the Holy Spirit as He fills His role on earth. The Holy Spirit indwells us. The Spirit of holiness can and will be our guide as we attempt to achieve God's command to be holy as He is holy. Since scripture specifically identifies this spirit, don't be afraid to ask for spiritual help from Him.

Create in me a clean heart, O God, and renew a steadfast spirit within me. (Psalm 51:10)

Restore to me the joy of Your salvation, and sustain me with a willing spirit. (Psalm 51:12)

Steadfast spirit, willing spirit

Here we find another God-given spirit. This is a spirit tool to help us live a full and abundant life in Him.

In the beginning of this unit, I indicated that we were going to talk about three types of spirits and their role in our walk with Christ: (1) God-sent spirits; (2) the spirit of, or in, man; and (3) evil or satanic spirits. I have intentionally not touched much on God's Holy Spirit or the spirit of man.

These two spirits are identification of characteristics that God wants to see manifested in the spirit of man. Willingness and steadfastness are mentioned in various forms in the Bible. Steadfastness could be considered to be one of the fruits of the Spirit and should be thought of in that context. Sometimes we need to ask and receive help in an area, and other times we have to change our minds. In this case, it would be a quality decision that since I have committed my life to Christ, I am going to be always willing to do His will. Decide it, do it. Seek a steadfast spirit.

God has also supplied a willing spirit, which will help us in this walk. Like the others, we have to be willing to receive it. Why are we so much more willing to accept the evil spirits than those from God?

Spirit of Truth

> … That is the Spirit of truth, whom the world cannot receive, because it does not see Him or know Him, but you know Him because He abides with you and will be in you. (John 14:17)

I see this Spirit of Truth as a God-given aid. Who is "the way, the truth, and the life"? The Anointed One, the Lord, our Savior and our Redeemer. The indwelling Spirit of Truth is used here instead of the term Holy Spirit. The application? Since He dwells in you, communicate with Him as a distinct part of the Godhead. Talk to Him, talk about Him. He is the one who makes faith an action word in your life.

When you are in ministry and you cast out a controlling, lying, and deceitful spirit, fill the vacancy by inviting the Spirit of Truth in the name of Jesus.

Here we identify a spirit given by God that will empower us to more easily abide in and with the Anointed One. He is the way, the truth, and the life. God offers us the Spirit of Truth to help accommodate us in the enormity of Christ's indwelling Holy Spirit.

Discussion Topics from Unit 12

According to Exodus 28:3, what spirit did God want in His craftsmen?

According to Ephesians 1:17, who was the giver of the spirit of wisdom?

Romans 1:4 mentions what spirit?

John 14:17 mentions what spirit?

Who can receive that spirit?

Unit 13

More about Helping Spirits

> But having the same spirit of faith, according to what is written, "I believed, therefore I spoke," we also believe, therefore we also speak. (2 Corinthians 4:13)

What an awesome sequence of God's power in the written word. In this verse, Paul opens by explaining that he has been given the spirit of faith. As mentioned earlier, this spirit is one we can loose or ask to come upon any individual, including ourselves, at any time.

He then goes right to the scripture they had at the time and quotes it, saying, "As it is written." After quoting the verse, he says (in my words), "Scripture says it, so I do it." In this instance, Paul's action was to speak. The teaching here is a call to action for any believer reading this letter of Paul's. He is saying to anyone of the faith (also in my words), "When the spirit of faith shows the believer something in God's Word, that something can and should be done by the believer."

We are saved by grace through faith. God chooses to make this faith available to all of us. It is a free gift. This Spirit of faith is His starter package to all Christians; it is also the "measure of faith" it takes to get us to believe and receive Jesus. Jesus is the gate into His power, His kingdom, His heaven, and His family.

> The Spirit of the Lord will rest on Him, the spirit of wisdom and understanding, the spirit of counsel and strength, the spirit of knowledge and the fear of the Lord. (Isaiah 11:2)

In this prophecy from Isaiah, the Spirit of the Lord is resting upon the Messiah, the Anointed One. It is the Holy Spirit. Isaiah 11:1 makes that clear, because it talks about the Messiah, the Anointed One, springing from the roots of Jessie. Of course Jesus's lineage came through David who was the son of Jessie.

The verses following 1 and 2 describe how Jesus will use the spirits of wisdom, understanding, counsel, strength, knowledge, and fear of the Lord to perform His earthly work. We sometimes talk about the task of equipping the saints. Jesus was spiritually, physically, and intellectually equipped for ministry when His ministry began. Those same spirits that equipped Jesus for His ministry are still available to equip us today.

How often have you said to God, "Lord help me; I don't understand this"? How about just asking Jesus to set free, to assist you, the spirit of understanding? Spiritual help is critical to living a successful life here.

Spirit of Counsel

Claiming that Jesus is our advocate forever is scriptural. Praise God He is on our side. He can and will loosen this advisor, the Spirit of Counsel, for us anytime we ask and accept it. One of the concepts of spiritual warfare is that of binding and loosing as Jesus taught in Mathew 16:19. In its simplest form, the believer binds or disables Satan's spiritual agent and loosens one of God's spirits to replace it. God allows us to refuse His counsel. Life might work better for us if we accepted and followed His counsel more than we do. God will deliver His counsel to us in whatever way He chooses. He may simply have a person tell us. The counsel may come as a thought, from a book, or from observing His creation. His counsel will always agree with His written Word, the Bible.

Spirit of Strength

If you are not using this one, you are probably unique! Nearly everyone at some time in their life reaches a point where they don't feel as if they have what it takes to get through a situation. Get the help! Strength is near you. Loosen the spirit of strength and receive it. Do it by, and in the name of, Jesus. A prayer for that might sound like this: "Father, according to your

Word, there is a Spirit of Strength. I am too weak for this situation. Please empower me with your Spirit of Strength in the name of Jesus."

Earlier, we looked at the gates the enemy uses to attack us. Our senses—our eyes, ears, noses, mouths, and our very skin—are gates that respond to either good or bad stimulation. Isaiah 28:6 tells us of a God-given strength to "repel the onslaught at the gates." That is exactly where we need to have and apply the Spirit of Strength. We need to ask God for the Spirit of Strength to repel the enemy as he approaches the gates to our soul.

Spirit of the Fear of the Lord

I, like many other believers, have struggled with what the correct attitude is concerning fear of the Lord. Some teach this as being the kind of fear generated by the Old Testament God who did not hesitate to tell His people to kill all the enemies—men, women, children, and animals. He even carried this to the degree of demanding death for rebellious children among His people. Before the death and resurrection of Jesus, there was no deliverance from sin, so death was the way to eliminate it. Jesus bore all of that rot on the cross. Reverential trust, including the hatred of evil, is a suitable understanding of fear of the Lord in this age of grace. Reverence will put a person on their face in front of God as quickly as fear. It was out of reverence that Moses took his shoes off when he was on holy ground. It was out of reverence Jesus said, "Thy will be done" when He knew God's will and knew He could have avoided the cross.

This unit leads us in the examination of spirits in the kingdom of darkness. How do they impact us? Some of the scriptures we will be looking at identify not only the evil spirit but a godly substitute we can use to replace them. In other instances, a godly replacement was not included. Those passages will be managed as we come to them.

Isaiah identifies the first evil spirit to be examined in this unit.

> The Spirit of the Lord God is upon me; because the Lord hath anointed me to bring good news to the afflicted; He hath sent me to bind up the broken-hearted, to proclaim liberty to captives, and freedom to prisoners; to proclaim the favorable year of the Lord and the day of vengeance of

our God; to comfort all who mourn, To grant those who mourn in Zion. Giving them a garland instead of ashes, The oil of gladness instead of mourning, The mantle of praise instead of a spirit of fainting, so they will be called oaks of righteousness, the planting of the Lord, that he may be glorified. (Isaiah 61:1–3)

This verse opens talking about bringing good news to the afflicted, and it lists a few afflictions. Specifically listed are those who have lost their liberty, their freedom, and are brokenhearted and mourning. I have observed in today's society addictions are frequently afflictions! In light of this Isaiah verse, it is noteworthy that the outcomes of addictions when they have run their course are broken hearts, loss of liberty, loss of freedom, and mourning. Praise the Lord. He is the answer.

The "spirit of fainting" referred to here is similar to the spirit of fear or timidity referred to in 2 Timothy 1:7. That verse also mentions a spirit of power, of love, and of a sound mind or discipline.

For God has not given us a spirit of timidity, but of power and love and discipline. (2 Timothy 1:7)

I was blessed with an aunt who lived a full and abundant life for more than a hundred years. I remember her commenting in her later years that we as a nation are teaching our children they should live in fear. She was right.

A young father we knew a few years ago is a good example of that. As his daughter was learning to walk, he was nearly constantly telling his baby girl, "Don't fall!" and "Watch out!" There was a continuous string of "be careful" statements covering her every growing-up venture. We never heard a statement from the father urging enjoyment or victory or encouraging her to take a risk. Her worldview will likely forever be swayed by that parental input.

The world should be able to tell the difference between when a person is a nonbeliever and when that same person becomes a believer. Fainting, timidity, and fear are all names of spirits whose job is to keep believers from meeting the scriptural command of boldness. They are listed as evil spirits, and a Christian should not accept their influence. The heathens, the Gentiles, should be able to tell the difference. The given names of the spirits (fear, timidity, etc.) aptly identify traits that keep us from setting ourselves apart from the world system. They discourage us from displaying our relationship with the risen Lord.

A biblical example of this discouragement is found in John 3. Nicodemus went to see Jesus by night, displaying his timidity. He didn't want to be seen talking with Jesus in the light of day and had to overcome a whole lot of fear to muster the courage to go seek out Jesus under the cover of darkness. Nicodemus became much bolder after he met Jesus face to face.

We can be bold, we can operate in power, and we can control our thought life. Satan has only as much power over us as we choose to allow him to have.

So what's the application? Don't be afraid as a believer to bind and cast out a spirit of fear or timidity in the name of Jesus and to let loose the spirit of power, love, and a sound mind in the person. It is as simple as saying the words, directly addressing the evil spirit as Jesus did. Just say, "Spirit of fear, I command you to leave this person in the name of Jesus." Do not attempt a conversation. Upon implementation of that command, loosen the spirit of love, power, and a sound mind to fill the vacancy left by the previous command. Remember you are doing what you were taught and what the Word says.

The next verse continues to move us from fear, from slavery, into liberation and adoption. It is not such a big step as it seems at first glance.

> For you have not received a spirit of slavery leading to fear
> again, but you have received a spirit of adoption as sons by
> which we cry out, "Abba! Father!" (Romans 8:15)

We can stop and pitch our tent here for a while. These are a few short lines with four important truths in them.

First truth: There is a spirit of slavery. It does exist. It is more real than a couple of words in the memory bank of your computer. As a child, I remember smokers being referred to as nicotine slaves. Slavery is equivalent to being in bondage! Being in bondage means you are not making the decisions in your life. It also implies that life is not the way you want it to be. Jewish slavery in Egypt was called bondage. We are in bondage to anything or anyone that controls us without our permission.

Second truth: Bondage leads to fear, and fear stifles boldness. There is a spirit of fear that exists and lurks among us; we looked at it in the previous section. But we don't have to have it! Cast it out, rebuke it, replace it, and avoid the broken snare of bondage.

Third truth: There is a God-given spirit of adoption. It will replace the spirit of slavery. How does that work? You, of your own free will, place yourself under the care of Jesus Christ by allowing Him control of your life. You make Him Lord (boss) of your life, becoming His bondservant. During the period of time the "new world" of America was being settled, people often learned a trade by becoming an apprentice. Usually this was for an agreed-to amount of time. There was no pay beyond what it took to keep the person alive. The apprentice, of his own free will, agreed to become this person's slave or servant. It was known as indentured servant. The agreement bound the person into service. God likes to see this level of commitment to Him forever, so He adopts you into His family. He calls you and treats you as a son or daughter.

Fourth truth: We end up calling God our daddy! What a remarkable sequence. Since you cannot serve two masters, you are now in a winning situation as long as you do not decide to allow anything else to have lordship in your life.

Discussion Topics from Unit 13

According to 2 Corinthians 4:13, what spirit caused Paul to speak?

Use Isaiah 11:2 to make a list of the spirits mentioned in the verse.

What does the spirit of slavery lead to?

What good spirit is mentioned here?

Unit 14

Introducing the Full Armor of God

In the physical world, one of the myriad responsibilities parents have is teaching kids to dress appropriately for conditions. Having been raised in the upper Midwest in a bygone time, going outside came with a set of questions or instructions.

In the winter, it was:
"Do you have your mittens?"
"Put your ear flappers down."
"Buckle up your four-buckle overshoes."
"Don't put your tongue on the pump handle."

In the summer it became:
"Don't go swimming until an hour after you have eaten."
"Wear a shirt some of the time so you don't sunburn."
"Don't wear your shoes unless we are going to town."

All the instructions had a physical or economic reasoning. Under the worst of winter conditions, the way one was dressed could be a matter of life or death.

Our God has alerted us to the dangers in the spiritual world. When we become cognizant of the battles and battleground of spiritual warfare, we see the potential for needing some protection. God started this with Adam and Eve. When sin endangered them physically and spiritually, he made garments to protect them. In the spiritual realm, He has told us to put on the full array of armor for the battle. It is free. He furnishes it. It is important that we explore this God-provided protection before entering deeper into a study on the subject of spiritual warfare. Under the worst of spiritual conditions, this battle could be a matter of life and death.

> Finally, be strong in the Lord and in the strength of His might. Put on the full armor of God, so that you will be able to stand firm against the schemes of the devil. For our struggle is not against flesh and blood, but against the rulers, against the powers, against the world forces of this darkness, against the spiritual forces of wickedness in the heavenly places. (Ephesians 6:10–12)

These first three verses are a quick look at the struggle we are in. They tell us who it is with and where its source is. These verses and subjects are explored in depth in this study. The next verse starts telling us what to wear in the battle.

> Therefore, take up the full armor of God, so that you will be able to resist in the evil day, and having done everything, to stand firm. (Ephesians 6:13)

He says that we are to take up the armor; we are to put it on. He starts verse 13 with "Therefore." He is telling us that because this will happen, get ready for it. Only then will we be able to resist, be able to stand firm.

Spiritual warfare is not something we can hide from. Fighting in it requires faith, a belief in God and His Word. He is not going to put this armor on us. He is saying to us, "Here it is; put it on."

> Stand firm therefore, having girded your loins with truth, and having put on the breastplate of righteousness, and having shod your feet with the preparation of the gospel of peace; in addition to all, taking up the shield of faith with which you will be able to extinguish all the flaming arrows of the evil one. And take the helmet of salvation, and the sword of the Spirit, which is the word of God. With all prayer and petition pray at all times in the Spirit,

and with this in view, be on the alert with all perseverance
and petition for all the saints. (Ephesians 6:14–18)

In the following units, we will be exploring how to put on and function with His equipment. The equipment in His armor consists of:

1. Truth (girdle)
2. Righteousness (breastplate)
3. The gospel of peace (shoes)
4. Faith (shield)
5. Salvation (helmet)
6. The Word (sword)

Put on your armor and continue on. Never take it off. Check it daily. It is essential to know how to put on the full armor and keep it functional.

We had the opportunity to visit the United Kingdom a few years ago. Our first breakfast in the UK was in Liverpool. Only my wife and I were at the table when the waitress came. We were not world travelers. We had no one guiding us through the little eccentricities that were unique to this marvelous culture we were visiting. We asked the waitress for breakfast advice. She suggested the full English breakfast. It was the whole works. It was large quantities of everything we could want for breakfast. It exceeded our expectations and was more than adequate.

God's full armor is large quantities of anything and everything one needs to make it through the day. It is more than adequate. In the book of Galatians, Paul uses different words to make the same point.

For all of you who were baptized into Christ have clothed
yourselves with Christ. (Galatians 3:27)

This verse from Galatians tells us that we have already "clothed" ourselves in Christ. That is the covering of righteousness that was lost in the garden. When we are clothed in Christ, we have put on His righteousness.

We need to look at Ephesians 6:10, 11, 12, and 13 to see why we should bother to put on the full armor. It is not to cover nakedness. It is not for comfort. It is not for looks. Verse 10 says the armor will make us strong with the power of His might.

Verse 11 says it will make us able to stand up against the devil's wiles. Verses 12 and 13 tell us it will make us able to stand against the enemy. Those are good reasons to put on God's armor.

The armor God provides for us is personalized. David found this out when Saul tried to outfit David in his, Saul's, armor. First Samuel gives an account of when David tried to put on Saul's armor.

> Then Saul clothed David with his garments and put a bronze helmet on his head, and he clothed him with armor. David girded his sword over his armor and tried to walk, for he had not tested them. So David said to Saul, "I cannot go with these, for I have not tested them." And David took them off. (1 Samuel 17:38–39)

We need to have the correct armor for the giant we are fighting. At the beginning of this account, Saul tried to get David to wear his personal physical armor rather than God's spiritual armor and weapons. David did not test the armor King Saul wanted him to use. It fit David so poorly that he was unable to walk while wearing it. If walking in it was impossible, he certainly didn't want to do battle with a giant while wearing it.

In every facet of our Lord's relationship with us, He treats us as unique individuals. His full armor for you and me is more individually suited than worldly clothing made by the finest tailor. Although your spiritual armor will have the same six elements as everyone else's and will be as effective as everyone else's, they won't be the same. God did not create us with a cookie cutter, and He will not outfit us with one. God's armor fits perfectly.

The first verse in this selection was Ephesians 6:10. It told us we must be strong enough to take the armor into battle. It also said it would be by the strength of the Lord. This is the same Lord, the same God, who provided strength, wisdom, and courage to David. David was sure he was on the side of righteousness. We need to learn to have the same peace and assurance in our battles as David had in this one.

In the book of Nehemiah, he and his countrymen were working on the wall in Jerusalem. They were under constant threat by a very real enemy. He tells us about some of their response in chapter 4.

From that day on, half of my servants carried on the work
while half of them held the spears, the shields, the bows
and the breastplates; and the captains were behind the
whole house of Judah. (Nehemiah 4:16)

These workers had no intent of letting the enemy frustrate the work
they were doing for their God. Their attitude was much the same as
David's. They had an assurance that they were doing the work desired by
the Creator God. They were just as sure that any battle would result in a
victory for them. Having said that, why did they have breastplates, spears,
shields, and bows with them all the time? The answer is simple. That was
what God provided for them. He provided physical protection needed in
a physical battle. Those things were needed to protect them from physical
damage. They were to ward off attacks from a frustrated enemy.

That is exactly why we are told to put on the full armor. It is spiritual
protection for a spiritual battle. It will ward off attacks from a frustrated
spiritual enemy. It will protect the work of God being done in us and
around us.

Put on the full armor of God, so that you will be able to
stand firm against the schemes of the devil. (Ephesians 6:11)

This is a repeated verse. Verse 13 says nearly the same thing. When
God repeats an instruction, it is time to take heed. He is conveying a
message of urgency or importance. We need to be able to sustain our
position against the enemy, or he will be able to control us. The purpose
of this Ephesians chapter 6 passage is to teach us how to live in the battle
and how to live in the victory.

Notice the difference between what one would stand firm against in
spiritual warfare compared to physical warfare. During World War II,
a famous example of standing firm was during the Battle of the Bulge.
When the German commander offered to accept surrender terms from
the American commander, the one-word written response he received
was "Nuts." There would be no surrender to men, tanks, and artillery.
They stood firm. They stood firm in the dead of winter. They stood firm

with a shortage of ammunition, food, and air support. They overcame by doggedly standing firm while the enemy was trying to kill them.

But look at what verse 11 says we should stand firm against. We are to be equipped to stand firm against the schemes of the devil. In the natural world, we can't even see a scheme. In the flesh, we don't know the devil is calling on us to surrender or die. What a different war we are in. In the spiritual war, we can put ourselves in bondage and not know what we are doing. So the Word says we can "stand firm." According to scripture, how do we stand firm?

> Submit therefore to God. Resist the devil and he will flee
> from you. (James 4:7)

In the book of James, standing firm looks like submitting to God first and then resisting the devil and gaining victory. The action words here are "submit," "resist," and "flee." Who does the submitting? The believer does. Who does the resisting? You! The child of God submits and resists. Who flees? The devil—the one who was doing the attacking is the one who must leave in defeat.

The Belt of Truth

> Those who were rebuilding the wall and those who carried
> burdens took their load with one hand doing the work and
> the other holding a weapon. (Nehemiah 4:17)

The book of Nehemiah demonstrates what it means to be continually prepared for battle with the enemy. God's people were working with one hand and ready to battle the adversary with the other hand. When does Satan like to attack us? The answer is *anytime*. He is there when we are busy, working, playing, or just plain bored. Rarely does he attack when we are expecting it. We tend to become complacent and lulled into a state of security that is not realistic. When that happens, we may forget to bring the armor with us and become extremely vulnerable to his schemes.

> For our struggle is not against flesh and blood, but against
> the rulers, against the powers, against the world forces of

this darkness, against the spiritual forces of wickedness in
the heavenly places. (Ephesians 6:12)

When Paul says we are not fighting against flesh and blood, he is
telling us this battle is not in what we call the normal realm, the realm
that we experience with our five senses. He tells us we are warring against
real but invisible enemies in a battle that has been won but, for individuals,
has not been finished. He describes the different levels of control or what
could be seen as the hierarchy in the spirit realm: rulers, powers, forces of
darkness, and wickedness. He states that the locations of these forces are
"heavenly places." This is a battle against Satan and his angels (imps or
demons). These are spirit beings—demons if you like. They are masters of
deception and scheming. Like Nebuchadnezzar, they want us to bow down
to their king. The full armor gives us the tools we need to win every time.
If we forget some or all of the armor, victory is rare.

Therefore, take up the full armor of God, so that you
will be able to resist in the evil day, and having done
everything, to stand firm. Stand firm therefore, having
girded your loins with truth, and having put on the
breastplate of righteousness. (Ephesians 6:13–14)

We will look at each piece of the armor. We will look at what it is, what
it does, how to put it on, and how to use it.

The first two pieces of the armor are addressed in Ephesians 6:14. He
uses the word "having" at the beginning of the dressing process. He is
telling us that when we are done with the process or have finished what He
is going to tell us, we must stand firm. The Bible does not give us specific
instructions such as "stand firm" if it is not an achievable and expected
outcome. I like to call the dressing in the armor process "putting on Jesus."

Have you ever watched construction workers while they are on the
job? Each of them wears a heavy leather belt. This belt is designed so that
all the tools the worker is going to need are suspended from the belt. Both
hands and feet are free to move about and transport construction items
as needed. Construction workers are like Nehemiah's workers; everything
they are going to need is within reach. This spiritual belt or girdle carries

the truth. It is worth noting that the belt or girdle of soldiers in Bible times provided protection for the reproductive organs. The first indication of mature Christians is the ability to reproduce themselves. The last thing Satan wants is more new Christians.

How does one get into this belt of truth? One must first settle in his or her heart, soul, and mind what is the truth. The Truth I will follow, and where I will look for direction every time, is this.

> I will ask the Father, and He will give you another Helper, that He may be with you forever; that is the Spirit of truth, whom the world cannot receive, because it does not see Him or know Him, but you know Him because He abides with you and will be in you. (John 14:16–17)

This "Helper" that Jesus promised to give us and has given us is also called the Spirit of Truth. Jesus has made it clear that the Helper is the Holy Spirit. This Holy Spirit, this Spirit of Truth, indwells us and empowers us. It is vital to understand and receive this third Person of the Godhead as a part of the new creature we become when we decide to follow Jesus. The Holy Spirit directs us.

> And the Word became flesh, and dwelt among us, and we saw His glory, glory as of the only begotten from the Father, full of grace and truth. (John 1:14)

> I and the Father are one. (John 10:30)

> Jesus said to him, "I am the way, and the truth, and the life; no one comes to the Father, but through Me." (John 14:6)

When Jesus said in John 10, "the Father and I are one," He meant that He and God are one, sharing the same traits. If God is love, then Jesus is love as well. If one of them is described as truth, then they both are. In John 14, the Holy Spirit is referred to as "the Spirit of Truth." This is the Spirit who indwells us and empowers us during our stay on this earth. The trinity then is the fullness of this trait we are to put on.

We are blessed now to have the truth in a tangible written form. To get this concept solidified in your mind and spirit, I suggest a reread of the four scripture readings from the book of John, which precede this commentary.

How does one put on this belt of truth? Here we are, facing an unseen enemy, and yet the outcome of the battle is often visible. The loss of the spiritual battle that is in our mind can and will (if we lose it) lead to sin. Sin can and will eventually have fleshly outcomes. We can get a clue about how to correctly gain the protection of the belt of truth by reading Romans 10:10–13 and verse 17. These verses hammer on the importance of our actions and our confession. The action is believing in the heart (sometimes thought of as faith) and confessing with the mouth (which is an action based on faith). Action empowers faith. Those verses point toward righteousness and salvation, but the principles of believing and confessing thread through the Bible like a superhighway to victory.

When a person can say he or she accepts and believes in his or her heart that God the Father, Jesus the Son, and the Holy Spirit are the fullness of truth, and the Bible is the written version, that person will have the belt of truth. If any of those fundamental beliefs are not accepted, the belt could slip down around the ankles when needed the most. The belt, the truth, holds everything else in place.

To put on the belt of truth, start the day with this prayer or one of your own:

> *Thank you, my Lord, for showing me the truth about yourself. Thank you for reminding me that you are the only God, the Creator of Heaven and Earth, the King of the Universe, my father who loves me, and my Shepherd who leads me. You are my wisdom, my counselor, my hope, and my strength. You are all I need today.*

Breastplate of Righteousness

The second part of the armor is also listed in Ephesians 6:14. Paul called it the "breastplate of righteousness." We have an updated version of this breastplate for today's military, police, and quarterbacks on football teams. That protective layer is called "body armor" or sometimes a "flak jacket." What does it do? It provides a degree of protection from explosive devices, bullets, and sharp objects that could kill or maim.

Kill or maim is just what the devil wants to do to us. In the case of the football quarterback, that layer protects him from flying four-hundred-pound defensive linemen who are trying to maim him. There are new materials being developed all the time to make these protective devices lighter, cooler, stronger, more durable, and provide still more protection.

Our breastplate is the same as it was a couple of thousand years ago. Where do we get stuff like righteousness with which to construct our protection? It helps to think of justification as an act and think of righteousness as a condition.

> For all have sinned and fall short of the glory of God, being justified as a gift by His grace through the redemption which is in Christ Jesus. (Romans 3:23–24)

We have all fallen short. None of us are or ever have been justified and/or redeemed by earning it. Those two elements, the elements of gifting and grace, need to be in place for godly righteousness to happen. How were those two elements supplied? "By grace which is in Christ Jesus." The next verse touches on what grace is. Read it carefully, reflecting on what each word or phrase is saying.

> Now to the one who works, his wage is not [credited] as a favor, but as what is due. But to the one who does not work, but believes in Him who justifies the ungodly, his faith is [credited] as righteousness. (Romans 4:4–5)

Righteousness is apart from works. It is paid for; it is given. Righteousness is imputed; faith is the only prerequisite. Faith comes from God and is gifted as well. Things that are given to us in the flesh or in the spirit usually have to be received or are of little use. When we get to Romans 10, we will see the simplest way to receive our righteousness. First, we need to see how it was achieved. We need to give the glory, honor, and praise to God.

> For if by the transgression of the one, death reigned through the one, much more those who receive the abundance of grace and of the gift of righteousness will reign in life through the One, Jesus Christ. (Romans 5:17)

Sin and death were the results of mankind's disobedience, as was demonstrated by Adam and Eve. The apostle Paul explains in Romans five that the abundance of grace needed and the gift of righteousness we must have are already provided by the Lord Jesus Christ. He bought and paid for this breastplate of our righteousness. It is perfect and without blemish because of grace. It fits us!

> For the wages of sin is death, but the free gift of God is eternal life in Christ Jesus our Lord. (Romans 6:23)

The outcome of sin is death, eternal separation from God our Creator. Sin is a manifestation of unrighteousness. Jesus cut though, cleansed, and removed the sin so He could clothe us in Himself and His righteousness to present to our Father. Before Adam and Eve sinned in the garden, they had no need for this breastplate. They were created in the image of a righteous God. They were clothed in righteousness. It was when sin came in that righteousness disappeared. From then until the death and resurrection of Jesus, the condition of righteousness was a scarce commodity.

> ... For with the heart [a person] believes, resulting in righteousness, and with the mouth he confesses, resulting in salvation. (Romans 10:10)

If anyone chooses to believe to the very core of his being that Jesus is who He says He is, then righteousness moves in. It is imputed by the Holy Spirit. It is planted in us. If that belief is followed by verbal acknowledgment, then salvation is sealed and affirmed forever in the believer. We receive our salvation as a gift because of faith and grace, which are also gifts. Believe it with all your heart! This is the same verse that taught us how to put on the belt of truth. Believing, receiving, and confessing are access routes to each part of God's armor.

> I have been crucified with Christ; and it is no longer I who
> live, but Christ lives in me; and the life which I now live in
> the flesh I live by faith in the Son of God, who loved me
> and [gave] Himself up for me. I do not nullify the grace
> of God, for if righteousness comes through the Law, then
> Christ died needlessly. (Galatians 2:20–21)

Christ died for our righteousness. It is ours! Righteousness was forfeited in the garden. It was purchased, bought back, for an incomprehensible price. That buying back happened thousands of years later. There was a garden involved in the redemption of God's people as well. Jesus was praying in the garden when they came to arrest Him.

> More than that, I count all things to be loss in view of
> the surpassing value of knowing Christ Jesus my Lord,
> for whom I have suffered the loss of all things, and count
> them but rubbish [so] that I may gain Christ, and may
> be found in Him, not having a righteousness of my own
> derived from the Law, but that which is through faith in
> Christ, the righteousness which comes from God on the
> basis of faith, that I may know Him and the power of His
> resurrection and the fellowship of His sufferings, being
> conformed to His death. (Philippians 3:8–10)

We have the hope of counting all the things of this world as rubbish. We have the assurance of righteousness because it comes from God by the avenue of faith. Christ Jesus, my Lord—the key word being Lord. Without going into my testimony, I must acknowledge trusting Christ in a life-changing way was a decision I made at the age of thirty-seven, in November 1972. In 1995, twenty-three years later, I was working as a social worker. During a staff meeting, our supervisor asked me where I had received my "soft skills" training. She was referring to abilities to work effectively with people in need. I responded with the truth. I said, "They were imputed in 1972." Sadly, that ended the discussion.

Our righteousness is imputed. The same God that imputes needed skills or talents imputed the righteousness of His only Son into us. He made that available through His grace and His faith, yet we have to receive. Our response should be a disciplined effort to live the way we are called to live. Our calling is to be holy because He is holy.

To put on the breastplate of righteousness, start the day with this prayer or one of your own:

> *Thank you, Father, for showing me the truth about myself—that, on my own, I could never be good enough to live in your presence. Thank you for taking my sins to the cross and offering me your righteous life. Lord, show me any sin that I need to confess right now, so nothing will hinder me from being filled to overflowing with your Holy Spirit. [You may need to take a little time here for some confessing.] Thank you for forgiving me and for filling me with your righteous life.*

Discussion Topics from Unit 14

According to John 14:6, how does one come to the Father?

According to Ephesians 6:14, what are the first two pieces of armor we are to put on?

According to Ephesians 6:15, what are the next two items?

According to Ephesians 6:16, what does the shield of faith protect us from?

In your own words, how would you describe a flaming arrow or fiery darts?

Unit 15

The Full Armor of God, Part 2

The Sandals of Peace

> ... And having shod your feet with the preparation of the
> gospel of peace ... (Ephesians 6:15)

What carries the load of all the armor when we have put it on? Our feet.
Our feet are going to get us to wherever we are going. The message, the
gospel, the good news, is what keeps us going. It must be the good news
of the birth, life, death, burial, resurrection, and ascension as set forth in
God's Word. I will let Paul define the gospel for us using the same words
he used to tell the gospel to the Corinthians.

> Now I make known to you, brethren, the gospel which I
> preached to you, which also you received, in which also
> you stand ... (1 Corinthians 15:1)

A simple statement of the gospel helps in understanding Paul's
statement. What is referred to as the gospel does lead to peace. Later the
peace part of this verse is examined.

Paul says to the Corinthians that he has already preached this same
message, saying, "You have received this and you stand in it." But he is
going to repeat himself once more, this time in writing. This thought
of getting one's feet shod with the gospel correlates well with the earlier
statement of "standing" in it.

> … By which also you are saved, if you hold fast the word
> which I preached to you, unless you believed in vain. (1
> Corinthians 15:2)

What is this good news, this gospel that gets people right with God? What is it that brought peace with Him? What is it that brought these people to the place where Paul calls them "saved"? It is hearing, believing, and receiving the gospel as proclaimed by Paul. God wants His people standing in the middle of this gospel with both feet. He wants that commitment to be obvious to the world.

First Corinthians 15:1 uses the word "received." First Corinthians 15:2 uses the word "believed," and verse 3 uses "received" again. Those action words along with "confession" are essential to being on this journey with Jesus. John's gospel, in chapter one, verses 11 and 12 assert this same point.

> For I delivered to you as of first importance what I also
> received, that Christ died for our sins according to the
> Scriptures. (1 Corinthians 15:3)

Paul starts with the fact that Jesus Christ did what no one else could do. He paid the perfect sacrifice for our sins. He did it just as the prophets had foretold. The fact that people of God accurately foretold the events that took place during the time Christ walked the earth adds credibility to His deity. Some of the prophecies were given thousands of years before He came to earth. This sacrificial death on the cross, for the sins of the world, is where our freedom from Satan's power of sin and death was broken. The darkness and fear were replaced with living hope and light.

> … And that He was buried, and that He was raised on the
> third day according to the Scriptures. (1 Corinthians 15:4)

Also, just as the prophets had foretold, He rose from the dead. He did this after having been dead and buried three days. This event of being eternally brought back from the dead achieved for our Lord and Savior a position over the entire universe. It is an eternal position that scriptures tell us is higher than all other positions.

… And that He appeared to Cephas, then to the twelve.

In verse five, Paul begins to talk about the people who had been there for the full duration of this happening. He introduces them as one would introduce witnesses in a courtroom. Why is the proclamation of the gospel so important? Paul explains that in first Corinthians.

> For if I preach the gospel, I have nothing to boast of, for I am under compulsion; for woe is me if I do not preach the gospel. (1 Corinthians 9:16)

Why did Paul preach the gospel? Verse 16 says he is under compulsion, that he is being driven. The gospel is not something to be hidden. The gospel should be on display in me. To quote Paul, "Woe is me if I do not preach the gospel." In Paul's life, as in our lives, to know the truth and not proclaim it should be impossible.

> For if I do this voluntarily, I have a reward; but if against my will, I have a stewardship entrusted to me. (1 Corinthians 9:17)

Paul knows that if he preaches the gospel voluntarily, there will be a reward. For Paul, as for all of us, the reward of proclaiming the gospel of Jesus is the privilege of doing it. We seldom hear someone say they were called to be a steward of the gospel, but Paul said it! Paul said he would do it if it were not his will. Involuntarily! Because he is an appointed steward, he is called and has been trusted with the calling to preach the gospel.

> What then is my reward? That, when I preach the gospel, I may offer the gospel without charge, so as not to make full use of my right in the gospel. For though I am free from all *men*, I have made myself a slave to all, so that I may win more. (1 Corinthians 9:18–19)

All of this is for the purpose of winning more people to Jesus.

Yes, Ephesians 6:15 told us to shod our feet with this gospel. How is that going to happen? First, we are going to get to learn what the gospel is. Paul spoke the gospel in a way that was easy and comfortable for him. We can imitate him and learn how God wants us to do it. We are not all gifted as evangelists, but we must all be ready to give reason for the hope that is within us. Paul also told Timothy how to handle the gospel.

> Therefore do not be ashamed of the testimony of our Lord, or of me His prisoner; but join with me in suffering for the gospel according to the power of God, who has saved us and called us with a holy calling, not according to our works, but according to His own purpose and grace which was granted us in Christ Jesus from all eternity. (2 Timothy 1:8–9)

Here Paul called it the "testimony of our Lord" rather than the gospel. How should the gospel be handled? It should be handled as a holy calling. We are to proclaim it without shame.

In summary, we are to be prepared, unashamed, and in holiness when we are equipped as a member of God's earthly army. In the context of Ephesians 6, this gospel we have been discussing is referred to as the gospel of peace. "Shod your feet with the preparation of the gospel of peace."

What do the scriptures have to say about this word peace?

> Therefore remember that formerly you, the Gentiles in the flesh, who are called "Uncircumcision" by the so-called "Circumcision," which is performed in the flesh by human hands—Remember that you were at that time separate from Christ, excluded from the commonwealth of Israel, and strangers to the covenants of promise, having no hope and without God in the world … and might reconcile them both in one body to God through the cross, by it having put to death the enmity. And He came and preached peace to you who were far away, and peace to those who were near. (Ephesians 2:11–12, 16–17)

During World War II, in the forty-eight United States, there were no hardships such as many nations suffered. There were shortages, and some things were unavailable. If someone complained about an issue, the common response was, "Don't you know there's a war on?"

We probably didn't know there was a war on when we first heard the gospel, but these verses say that we were at war with the law, yet Christ established peace for us. He made us one body at peace with God. Verse 17 says He came and offered peace. Peace is part of the gospel. It was what He preached. Christ abolished conflict with the law. In this age of grace. During this time since, Christ reconciled us by His grace, none of us should find ourselves at war with the law. If we find ourselves in this condition, it is because we have chosen to be there.

> For God is not a God of confusion but of peace, as in all
> the churches of the saints. (1 Corinthians 14:33)

There is a spirit of confusion, there is a spirit of conflict, and there is a spirit of peace. This gospel we are to spread is the gospel of peace. The message of the gospel carries with it the spirit of peace.

> Therefore, having been justified by faith, we have peace
> with God through our Lord Jesus Christ, through whom
> also we have obtained our introduction by faith into this
> grace in which we stand; and we exult in hope of the glory
> of God. (Romans 5:1–2)

What a sequence of events. We are justified by faith when we believe the words of the gospel. This justification through the work of Jesus restores us to righteousness so we can experience the work of righteousness, which is peace. Keep in mind that faith is an action word, and there are actions needed to put on the full armor. Following is a list of five things a person must do to put on the armor.

This is how to shod your feet with the gospel of peace:

1) Learn the gospel
2) Learn the Word

3) Learn your testimony
4) Learn to live in His peace
5) Learn to speak His words of peace

A prayer for the daily putting on the sandals of the gospel of peace:

> *God, I thank you for the peace you give me when I trust and follow you. Father, through your Holy Spirit indwelling me, teach me to learn and live the five steps of putting on the gospel of peace. Lord, it is the desire of my heart to stand firm at the right time and to walk with you, to grow, to love, to experience your peace. Show me how to help others find that peace.*

Shield of Faith

> In addition to all, taking up the shield of faith with which you will be able to extinguish all the flaming arrows of the evil one. (Ephesians 6:16)

One of the hymns of old is titled "Faith is the Victory." That hymn title is well grounded in the Bible. God has given us a shield of faith, and that shield protects us from the arrows of lies and deceit as well as any other subtle missiles the serpent sends our way. Peter gives us an intensive look at the protection of faith in 1 Peter, chapter 1. Peter jumps into this immediately in this letter.

> Blessed be the God and Father of our Lord Jesus Christ, who according to His great mercy has caused us to be born again to a living hope through the resurrection of Jesus Christ from the dead, to obtain an inheritance which is imperishable and undefiled and will not fade away, reserved in heaven for you, who are protected by the power of God through faith for a salvation ready to be revealed in the last time. (1 Peter 1:1–5)

We are protected by faith. Faith in God through His Son and His Spirit makes us ready for a salvation that is yet to be revealed. That same power of faith protects us now. That is the power of the shield. Luke records in chapter 6, verse 45 that a person speaks from what is in his heart. It is well for a Christian believer to pay attention to the words coming from his or her mouth. Are words of faith being spoken? Begin to think of speech as a sequence of statements of faith. That is my translation or summary of the second part of the verse. If our hearts our filled with faith, the words we speak reflect or mirror that faith. Unfortunately words like, "I think I am coming down with a cold" become a faith statement. Sometimes our words shoot holes in our shield.

> In this you greatly rejoice, even though now for a little while, if necessary, you have been distressed by various trials. (1 Peter 1:6)

We may get distressed with trials showing up in our lives. The distress is short lived as we experience trials and see them disappear in short order. We can rejoice when we see the futility of our enemy's efforts to defeat us. He is testing our full armor, and he is finding out how well protected we are. Rejoice!

> ... [So] that the proof of your faith, being more precious than gold which is perishable, even though tested by fire, may be found to result in praise and glory and honor at the revelation of Jesus Christ. (1 Peter 1:7)

We have a shield made of something more precious than gold. When those fiery arrows strike this shield of faith and are instantly extinguished, it brings glory, honor, and praise to God.

> And though you have not seen Him, you love Him, and though you do not see Him now, but believe in Him, you greatly rejoice with joy inexpressible and full of glory, obtaining as the outcome of your faith the salvation of your souls. (1 Peter 1:8–9)

Key words in this verse are "believe in Him." That is the essence of the protective faith we have been given—that faith brings joy inexpressible. The same grace-given faith that forms this shield is the combination that brought us into a peaceful relationship with our God. We get salvation through it!

> Hebrews 11:1
> Now faith is the assurance of things hoped for, the conviction of things not seen.

This verse is the commonly used biblical definition of faith. We have a highly effective invisible shield that we use to fight an unworldly war. It contains components of assurance that can also be expressed as confidence or certainty. In addition, there is an element of conviction, which means to fully trust. My favorite demonstration of faith comes from Abraham. It is recorded in the book of Romans.

> Without becoming weak in faith he contemplated his own body, now as good as dead since he was about a hundred years old, and the deadness of Sarah's womb; yet, with respect to the promise of God, he did not waver in unbelief, but grew strong in faith, giving glory to God, and being fully assured that what [God] had promised, He was able also to perform. (Romans 4:19–21)

The too old Abraham looked reality face-to-face and didn't flinch. God had promised him a son through Sarai. Nothing in his natural world could make him waver in his expectation. He did not let doubt show up at the entrance to his tent. His hope was a knowledge that the promise was going to happen. No fiery arrows were going to penetrate his world. With respect to God's Word, he was unwavering. He knew that if God said it, he could believe it. He didn't speak words of unbelief.

Like Abraham, when we do not waver in belief, our faith gets stronger. Our shield gets better. We don't get damaged by the arrows, and God gets the glory!

Verse 21 is one of those scripture verses that are so simple and so profound. Abraham was convinced that what God said He could do, and what He said He would do, it was going to happen. If God said it, God would perform it. That is an excellent definition of faith.

A prayer for daily putting on the shield of faith:

> *Thank you for giving me faith in you. I know I would be lost and separated from you for eternity without it. I know I couldn't earn it. Thank you that this shield you have given me works to perfection. I choose to believe in and count on everything you have shown me about yourself. I choose today to believe and accept everything you have promised me in your Word. Father, all I can give in return is praise, thanksgiving, and honor.*

Helmet of Salvation

And take the helmet of salvation, and the sword of the Spirit, which is the word of God. (Ephesians 6:17)

Faith and an honest appraisal of circumstances should be able to coexist. Abraham took an honest appraisal of his circumstances and then seems to say, "So what." Faith and unbelief sometimes are allowed to coexist. An old fashioned scriptural coming to Jesus will send unbelief scampering to a different domain.

This verse needs to be examined in two parts. One first must come an understanding that the battlefield of spiritual warfare is in the mind. That premise is examined in depth as we more closely examine the subject.

When Satan tempted Adam and Eve, he went through their minds to do it. When he tempted Jesus, he used logic and reasoning in his effort to persuade Him to sin. He has not changed his mode of operation. His tactics are still the same.

The unseen attacks are in the mind. If that invisible battle (in the mind) is won by the enemy, the results are often in the realm of the natural. They are visible. Where does the enemy attack to accuse, steal, and destroy? The mind.

What skills can we develop in the natural to help protect our mind from the spiritual attack? We can learn to pay attention to what influences we are allowing to access our mind. We can learn to become active listeners. One technique of active listening involves asking the speaker to repeat himself to make sure you heard correctly. The point of this is to screen what is going into one's mind. If something has been said that you know is opposite of God's Word, you can reject it. By becoming an active listener, we can repeat back, and we can say, "Did you say," "Do you mean," or "Will you clarify?" All of these techniques can help a person screen what is being accepted into his or her mind.

We are able to apply those same techniques to our thought life. We can become active thinkers. The Bible tells us if we have a vain imagination to not accept that thought. We are told to cast it down. We are to make a decision to not accept or dwell on ungodly thoughts. If you are experiencing a troubling thought, ask if it is today's trouble. If it doesn't deserve today's thoughts, it should be dismissed. The spiritual test for what one allows to enter his or her thought life is simple: Is it loving? Is it scriptural? Test all things. Hold what goes on in our mind to the standards we learn from scripture.

On the Richter scale of importance, nothing comes close to our salvation. Nothing has ever had a higher cost. Nothing has ever impacted eternity like our salvation impacts it. Salvation through Jesus Christ is now and forever. If we haven't received this free gift of salvation, the rest of this study is in vain. We won't be in the battle for Him. We will be on the side of evil, the side of the enemy. We must know of our salvation. The knowledge must be based on scripture rather than emotion. Presumption or assumption won't get that helmet of salvation on one's head either.

My wife and I have been blessed to live in what some might call an old-fashioned rural neighborhood. Close, caring relationships develop. They are common. When God captured us and led us into His salvation, our first response was to want to tell our families. The next step was to tell these friends and neighbors of many years or even many generations.

We started by inviting a couple for a meal. As lovingly as possible, we shared what had happened to us and told them this experience could be theirs. The woman of the couple became immediately angry. She informed us that she had been raised in a Christian home, her parents had always been Christian, and she had been insulted by what we said! That is what assumption and presumption look like when applied to nonbelievers. As that couple watched our changed lives over the following years, they became more open to hearing about Jesus.

Now is the time. Today is the day of salvation. Go to God with your own words. He knows your heart, so don't worry about the words. Tell Him you know you have sinned and fallen short of His glory. Tell Him you are ready to change your direction and follow Jesus wherever He takes you. Acknowledge that He paid the price of your redemption when He died. Acknowledge that you know you can't do this on your own. It is His grace. Then celebrate!

> For You will not abandon my soul to Sheol; nor will You allow Your Holy One to undergo decay. You will make known to me the path of life; in Your presence is fullness of joy; in Your right hand there are pleasures forever. (Psalm 16:10–11)

Who will God not allow to decay? Our Savior! He was out of the tomb in three days. The soul of the believer is not going to be abandoned either.

Eternal security! He will not abandon me. His presence is a joy, now and forever. Walking with Him forever is His plan for our life. Follow the path that Jesus sets before us. His joys and pleasures are everlasting.

Many people have had to learn Psalm 23. It seemed to be a part of our American heritage. Once again, on your own read, Psalm 23. It is about God. It is about you and me. It is about what He is doing. Then the passage changes from God-focused to you-focused. It is about the mind. It tells us God has us covered. We are protected.

When we make the decision to accept the free gift of salvation, the scriptures make it clear—we are children of God. God adopts us, and Jesus calls us His brothers and sisters. That is different from calling oneself a child of God just because he or she is a human dating back to Adam.

> See how great a love the Father has bestowed on us, that we should be called children of God; and such we are. For this reason the world does not know us, because it did not

know Him. Beloved, now we are children of God, and it has not appeared as yet what we will be. We know that, when He appears, we will be like Him, because we will see Him just as He is. And everyone who has this hope fixed on Him purifies himself. (1 John 3:1–3)

We will be like Jesus. We became more like Jesus when He gave us His Spirit. When He comes the second time, or when we go to be with Him, we will be like Him. What a promise!

This helmet of salvation is why we can be overcomers—because of the blood of Jesus and the word of our testimony. He gave His blood for us and gave our testimony to us. We only need to pray for salvation once. From that point on, it is a matter of confessing or acknowledging it. Therefore, the daily prayer will be an agreement or statement that it has happened.

A prayer for daily putting on the helmet of salvation:

> *Thank you for promising me salvation both for today's battles and for eternity.*

Discussion Topics from Unit 15

According to 1 Corinthians 15:5, who saw the resurrected Savior?

According to 2 Timothy 1–8, should a person be ashamed of his testimony?

According to Psalms 23:1, who is your shepherd?

According to Psalms 18:3, are we in danger from our enemies?

According to Psalm 40:11, what will God use to preserve you?

Unit 16

The Full Armor of God, Part 3

The Sword of the Lord

And take the helmet of salvation, and the sword of the Spirit, which is the word of God. (Ephesians 6:17)

The second part of the armor in Ephesians 6:17 in the NASB speaks of "the sword of the Spirit." Often it is called, "the sword of the Lord." It is referring to the Word of God. In Hosea 6:5 God says referring to His enemies, "I have slain them by the words of My mouth." Revelation 1:16, 2:12 and 19:15 reference Jesus and the sword. Genesis 1:3 says, "Then God said, 'Let there be light'; and there was light." Genesis has the first instance of God's Word. He spoke, He said it, and it happened. From Genesis through Revelation, the Word of God is presented with awe-inspiring power.

For the word of God is living and active and sharper than any two-edged sword, and piercing as far as the division of soul and spirit, of both joints and marrow, and able to judge the thoughts and intentions of the heart. (Hebrews 4:12)

This verse gives us a glimpse of the power of God's Word. He created the universe and its contents with His Word. He spoke, and it happened. His Word is living. It is active. It pierces. It divides. It can judge. His words all become verbs when spoken in faith. Actions take place as a result of His spoken Word. His words spoken in faith by believers still cause things to happen. They are still the truth. The truth spoken correctly causes change.

There are two definitions of God's word?

The written word is also known as *logos*. We use the word logo today in reference to branding or identifying a product. Logos is talking about the Bible. It is the infallible written Word of God. It is His divine expression or revelation to humanity. It was breathed by the Holy Spirit and written in response to that breathed Word. Jesus Christ is the fullness of this Word. When He walked on this earth, fully human and fully God, He was called the Word incarnate—the Word in the flesh.

> In the beginning was the Word, and the Word was with God, and the Word was God. He was in the beginning with God. All things came into being through Him, and apart from Him nothing came into being that has come into being … And the Word became flesh, and dwelt among us, and we saw His glory, glory as of the only begotten from the Father, full of grace and truth. (John 1:1–3,14)

Jesus Christ, the Anointed One, became the embodiment of the Word. When we are doing things in "the name of Jesus," we are bringing the whole of the Word to bear on the issue. When praying, we can't go wrong by praying God's Word back to Him.

The second word we use for the Word of God is *rhema*. The difference between these two words is how something is communicated. Rhema is the spoken Word of God, or "that which is or has been uttered by a human voice." Words spoken by the prophets are clear examples of the rhema Word.

When you are reading the Bible, and the written word says something to you other than the words that are in your reading that could be a rhema Word. Or you might be listening to a speaker speak about a specific verse, and you get a message even deeper or in addition to what the speaker is saying. That could be a rhema Word. A third example could be if you are reading scripture, and it "speaks" directly to a situation with which you have been struggling—that could be a rhema Word as well. We can and should also use these rhema Words as a sword to carry the battle to the enemy.

Can you see any dangers in using the rhema Word? Rhema Words must agree with the logos Word. What you are hearing must be supported and verified by the Bible.

A fundamentalist pastor friend of mine tells of being invited to a deliverance meeting that had been scheduled with a person who had need of it. At this point in his ministry, my friend could have been considered to be a skeptic about the whole process of deliverance. The person who invited my friend handled these encounters with the spoken Word and seldom referred to the Bible, which he had with him.

My friend reported listening as the meeting was happening and being surprised that every word this man used could be supported by scripture. I relate this incident as affirmation for the use of the spoken Word in personal ministry.

What do we do with the information we have been absorbing in this study? Is there an application? The Word of God is our weapon. We should use logos or rhema Words, speaking them with authority and confidence. We can speak them from memory, read them, or speak as the Holy Spirit leads.

For example: the devil is worrying me about finances. What could I speak? I could say that God will meet my needs according to His riches in Christ Jesus. I could say that because it is a close approximation of what the Bible says. I could state that I am not going to accept thoughts that are counter to God's word. You kind of slap the devil across the head with the sword of the Lord when you respond by speaking words of faith based on the written Word.

> And my God shall supply all your needs according to His riches in glory in Christ Jesus. (Philippians 4:19)

What is the catch? You have to know scripture or know where to find verses. You can't slay any dragons when you can't find your sword!

When you are feeling ill, you find what God says about that. Here are just two of many healing scriptures in the Bible. You don't need to find someone with "the gift of healing" to pray for you. You pray His Word back to Him. Tell Him you accept what His Word says about your illness.

> Who pardons all your iniquities, who heals all your diseases. (Psalm 103:3)

> And He Himself bore our sins in His body on the cross, [so] that we might die to sin and live to righteousness; for by His wounds you were healed. (1 Peter 2:24)

Not feeling so good? What do you say? The human response is, "Wow, I don't feel well. I think I am getting the flu." What could a spiritual response be? I could say aloud, "My sins are forgiven by the same person who heals all my diseases. Therefore, by faith, I am a well person on whom the enemy is trying to put a disease. I am not accepting." I might also say out loud, "By His wounds I am healed."

> And the tempter came and said to Him, "If you are the Son of God, command that these stones become bread." But He answered and said, "It is written, 'Man shall not live on bread alone, but on every word that proceeds out of the mouth of God.'" Then the devil took Him into the holy city; and he had Him stand on the pinnacle of the temple, and said to Him, "If You are the Son of God, throw Yourself down; for it is written, 'He will give (command) His angels charge concerning you'; and 'On their hands they will bear you up, [so that you will not] strike your foot against a stone.'" Jesus said to him, "On the other hand, it is written, 'You shall not put the Lord your God to the test.'" Again, the devil took Him to a very high mountain, and showed Him all the kingdoms of the world and their glory; and he said to Him, "All these things I will give You, if You fall down and worship me." (Matthew 4:3–9)

These verses are about the temptation of Jesus by Satan. They are examined in depth elsewhere in this study. I encourage the reader to review them, focusing on how the word is used there.

Satan used the Word of God to tempt Jesus. He consistently arrived at a wrong conclusion, and Jesus consistently responded with a correct usage of the Word. They fought with the Word. They both fought with a sword. What is the difference? Everything Satan uses is an imitation or a fake of the real thing that God has created. Jesus knew the Word, and He knew how to correctly use the sword. He converted the written Word to spoken. We can do that! We must do that to be protected in this battle. Spiritual battles, like fleshly battles, are not won with imitation or fake swords. To win it takes a real sword.

Rhema is the word used in "the sword of the Spirit, which is the word of God." The spoken word—Jesus spoke the written Word. He converted the written Word to spoken. We can do that! We must do that to be protected in this battle. That is how the sword of the Lord is used.

> And Jesus said to him, "If You can?" All things are possible to him who believes. (Mark 9:23)

All things are possible. The enemy here is unbelief. Unbelief makes faith statements like, "if you can" and "if you will." Faith statements say, "Your Word says …" and then quote scripture. Either of these statements is rewarded by its content!

> The sum of [Your] word is truth, and every one of [Your] righteous ordinances is everlasting. (Psalm 119:160)

The Word is truth, and it always will be. We can abide in it, and we are called to abide in it. We are able to live in His victory when we abide in it. Put on Jesus, crawl into His Word, pull it up over your head, and dwell in it.

> So Jesus was saying to those Jews who had believed Him, "If you continue in My word, then you are truly disciples of Mine; and you will know the truth, and the truth will make you free." (John 8: 31–32)

His Word takes us to the truth, and the truth sets us free. This could be called the sword of freedom. The days of spiritual bondage are gone.

> Death and life are in the power of the tongue, and those
> who love it will eat its fruit. (Proverbs 18:21)

Throughout this study, I stress the importance of what we are saying to God, to satan, to ourselves and to others. Are we speaking words of faith in God and overcoming? Or are speaking words that acknowledge defeat? Words have the power of life and death in them. We will be digesting the fruit of our tongue. What is the fruit you want to eat?

Today, military swords have become ceremonial. Even bayonets in combat have become a thing of the past. Swords are now used for show, for pomp and ceremony. People wearing swords probably have little idea of how to use them in accordance with their original purpose.

Can that happen with the Sword of the Spirit? Can the Word of God become a meaningless prop? Can the Bible sit on podiums unopened while great humanistic, motivational messages are presented? Can it be used to swear in government officials who might not be able to find the first page in the book? Has that happened in your life? Have you let God's Word become part of a private ceremony?

Swords were designed for cutting, for thrusting, and for clubbing. We should be using the Word of God for cutting, thrusting, and for clubbing the enemy every time, all the time.

There is nothing in the full armor we have examined that protects us from the rear. We are to be attacking the enemy and advancing. The Word of God must be in our hand and in our mouth.

A prayer for daily putting on the sword of the Spirit:

> *Thank you for the scripture you have given me. Please help me memorize them. Show me the one(s) you want me to use to overcome the lies and deceptions of the enemy to gain the victory in any battle I may face today.*

Discussion Topics from Unit 16

According to Hebrews 11:1, what is faith?

According to Romans 5:1–2, how are we justified?

According to Romans 3:23, what condition is common to all mankind?

According to 1 Corinthians 15:3, for what did Jesus die?

According to 1 Corinthians 15:4, what did they do with Christ?

Unit 17

Identifying the Counterfeits

> The end of all things is [near]; therefore, be of sound judgment and sober spirit for the purpose of prayer. (1 Peter 4:7)

This reference has been as an example of a verse that speaks about our human spirit and how we are to control it. "Sober" means being under correct control. Words like "serious," "reasonable," or "sedate" point to sound judgment and a sober spirit in a person correctly living the Word. When we are functioning as warriors for the kingdom of God, we should allow this spirit to influence us.

These next scriptures deal with why it is difficult at times to be on the right track when attempting to discern the difference between what a godly person should be doing and what he or she shouldn't be doing. It is about Daniel's ability to access an extraordinary spirit and use the outcome of that contact to glorify God.

> This was because an extraordinary spirit, knowledge and insight, interpretation of dreams, explanation of enigmas, and solving of difficult problems were found in this Daniel, whom the king named Belteshazzar. Let Daniel now be summoned, and he will declare the interpretation. (Daniel 5:12)

Daniel was gifted with an extraordinary spirit. God wanted him to be able to interpret dreams, foretell the future, and discuss the dead. The most important aspect of this account is that God would be glorified and His people protected. Paul tells his disciple to beware of "deceitful" spirits. These spirits will try to imitate God's spirits and will be hard to distinguish from the authentic one.

> But the Spirit explicitly says that in later times some will fall away from the faith, paying attention to deceitful spirits and doctrines of demons. (1 Timothy 4:1)

We have to be able to walk in the Spirit, knowing when and if we are listening to a Daniel spirit ordained by God or and when we are being led astray by deceitful spirits teaching the doctrines of demons. What does "falling away" look like, and how does it impact our life? As we look at various pertinent scriptures and apply them to situations, we should be able to answer that question.

God makes an original. Satan supplies a counterfeit. The devil makes a copy and tries to sell it as new and improved.

> As for the person who turns to mediums and to spiritists, to play the harlot after them, I will also set My face against that person and will cut him off from among his people. (Leviticus 20:6)

What do mediums, spiritualists, and diviners do? The things they do cause God to "set my face against" them. They interpret dreams, they foretell the future, they speak with the dead, and on and on. So who is the best liar, and what is the best lie? Of course, Satan gets the award as the best liar in the universe. Interesting, isn't it, that the God of the universe cannot lie, and the devil is the champion liar? So what does the best lie sound like? It is the one that sounds closest to the truth. The Timothy verse talks about making a decision to turn the wrong way, not through any trickery of the enemy but because we want to. Paul calls this, "falling away from the faith." The results are bad. Remember Saul? He purposefully decided to make a wrong turn with disastrous results.

> Now the Spirit of the Lord departed from Saul, and an
> evil spirit from the Lord terrorized him. (1 Samuel 16:14)

All of Saul's difficulties began much earlier. This evil spirit that was upon him drove him to what he did in the next verse. This sounds like a Job type of agreement; however, the difference here is that God withdrew His Spirit from Saul and apparently said to Satan, "Saul is no longer mine." The New Testament approximation of this is giving a person over to a depraved mind. In the first chapter of Romans, Paul talks about this process. The Romans' description closely parallels the mistakes Saul made. Verse 25 says, "They exchanged the truth of God for a lie." Verse 26 explains in detail how an unregenerate person can end up losing the battle he is in, and verse 28 makes it clear what becomes of that kind of person. The Word says they are without excuse. When God says that about a person, that person is close to being without hope.

King Saul played this out as if he had the same script the Romans had. Romans 1:28 tells the results of those bad decisions (to be examined in detail later in this book). God gave them over to do things that were not proper. One improper thing Saul decided to do is noted in 1 Samuel. Saul developed a plan whereby he could violate the law set forth in Leviticus 20:6. He decided to secretly access a sorceress.

Just like the self-destructing behaviors of this century, destruction didn't creep up on Saul. It took some slow, deliberate, bad decisions, and all those poor decisions started in his head. Saul had some help along the way. That help is the next demonic spirit with which I want to acquaint you—the spirit of jealousy, found named in the book of Numbers.

> … If a spirit of jealousy comes over him and he is jealous
> of his wife when she has defiled herself, or if a spirit of
> jealousy comes over him and he is jealous of his wife when
> she has not defiled herself … (Numbers 5:14)

That verse is an either/or verse. A spirit of jealousy will come over a person whether or not he or she has the defilement issue. I will examine some scriptural examples of how this can impact godly people. Satan will attack anyone. We will look at the account of his encounter with Jesus.

He attacks believers. He attacked the apostles. He will attack anyone, anywhere, anytime. We will continue to share how he tried to invade our family.

Spirit of Jealousy

> As they danced, they sang: "Saul has slain his thousands, and David his tens of thousands." Saul was very angry; this refrain displeased him greatly. "They have credited David with tens of thousands," he thought, "but me with only thousands. What more can he get but the kingdom?" And from that time on Saul kept a close eye on David. The next day an evil spirit from God came forcefully on Saul. He was prophesying in his house, while David was playing the lyre, as he usually did. Saul had a spear in his hand and he hurled it, saying to himself, "I'll pin David to the wall." But David eluded him twice. (1 Samuel 18:7–11 NIV)

What a great outcome of a battle. Saul and his army had won a major victory. The people of Saul's kingdom were praising God for the victory. They were giving Saul the credit he had earned. They were giving David credit for his efforts as a warrior in Saul's army. We, as readers who have the New Testament, talk about the need to die to self. Verse 8 points out what can happen if dying to self doesn't happen. Instead of Saul dying to self, eventually self was the death of Saul.

The words "self" and "ego" have connotations that generally mean someone is at the center of his own universe. The spirit of jealousy is linked to the spirit of fear. Saul states his fear, the source of his anger. The spirits of fear, jealousy, and anger are usually in the same place at the same time. Saul was afraid David was going to get control of the kingdom. He believed that fear, and he confessed that fear. That spirit of fear was brought on by the spirit of jealousy and opened the gate for anger. The resulting behavior? Lashing out. Unfortunately, this spirit commonly wants us to lash out at those who are closest to us. The physical manifestation of spiritual warfare has not changed. In the case of fear and jealousy, the outcome is the same today. Domestic violence is an example of today's outcome.

There is a common pattern demonstrated by this account. It starts with suspicion. In domestic violence today, the suspicion is verbalized as, "Where have you been? What were you doing? Where is my dinner? The process is called escalation and King Saul demonstrated it to a T. Suspicion matures into the spirit of jealousy, which festers into an angry spirit, which brings the victim to a spirit of fear. Unabated fear leads to violence. In today's homes it can be any abuse—verbal, sexual, physical, or self-destructive behavior such as substance abuse. Saul spent the last years of his life trying to kill a person who loved and respected him. It is lashing out from anger and fear, and that does not come from God.

David was completely sold out to Saul as king; he was supernaturally loyal. King Saul had just experienced an awesome victory on the battlefield, though, and the celebration did not please Saul. He became suspicious. The spirit of jealousy got in his head, and Saul responded to that spirit.

> Then Saul said to his servants, "Seek for me a woman who
> is a medium that I may go to her and inquire of her." And
> his servants said to him, "Behold, there is a woman who
> is a medium at En-dor." (1 Samuel 28:7)

He tells his men to go find a person who will help him break the Old Testament law. The culmination of all Saul's spiritual battles ends with very real physical outcomes. Buying in to Satan's lies that the battle is invisible and no one will know about it. That is what Saul did, and there were physical outcomes. That is what Adam and Eve did, and there were visible physical outcomes. That is how it works today too.

> Then Saul said to his armor bearer, "Draw your sword and
> pierce me through with it, [otherwise] these uncircumcised
> will come and pierce me through and make sport of me,"
> but his armor bearer would not, for he was greatly afraid.
> So Saul took his sword and fell on it. (1 Samuel 31:4)

Saul saw his sons killed; he saw his army being defeated. He saw himself wounded and humiliated. The king was a man without hope in this world. He couldn't even order his right-hand man to kill him. He had to kill himself. It all started in his head. It all started with bad decisions, decisions suggested by the enemy. He did lose his kingdom, but it wasn't because David or the people took it from him. What a contrast this is with the Daniel account: Daniel experienced moral, spiritual, and physically victorious outcomes. Saul suffered defeat in each of those realms.

King Nebuchadnezzar, who was a heathen, turned to Daniel, who was a man of God, for counsel, and God responded with honor. He honored Daniel as well as the heathen king. Saul, also a king, also a man chosen by God, turned for guidance to a woman of the world, a woman who was violating the law of the land at that time. She was violating God's law as well. God responded with dishonor to the king he had ordained. The truths taught in these examples are that God does not ordain and reward actions that violate His will and His Word.

We seem to be in a bit of a dilemma here. To our finite minds, it is hard to see much difference in what the two men did; one honored God, and one honored self.

There is a method of evangelism called "the Roman Way." It is an effective presentation of the gospel using the book of Romans. In the first chapter of Romans is a description of the way leading to depravity. King Saul managed to lead himself down this route.

> For even though they knew God, they did not honor Him as God or give thanks; but they became futile in their speculations, and their foolish hearts were darkened. (Romans 1:21)

The one positive in this verse is that the people referenced knew God. He was no stranger to them. An easy, seemingly innocent, first step in the searing process follows: they decided to not honor or thank Him. Not doing something God desires is a sin. They did not give God the credit, nor did they honor Him. They didn't bother to say thank you. When we practice not doing things a few times, suddenly the guilt that was there at the start is lessened. The searing process begins.

> Professing to be wise, they became fools, and exchanged the glory of the incorruptible God for an image in the

form of corruptible man and of birds and four-footed
animals and crawling creatures. (Romans 1:22–23)

And then the next step: it is cause and effect. They became fools. I
worked with a social worker who liked to use the phrase "the law of natural
consequences." In the Bible, I like to call them "if-then statements." If you
do X, then the result will be Y.

An if-then statement as it applies to this passage would be, if you
practice what is in verse 21, then the results are verse 22. It is simple to
become a fool in God's eyes; all one needs to do is to profess to be wiser
than God. Fools do dumb things.

Having become fools, they did foolish things. If we become fools, we
will, as they did in verse 23, give up the glory of God for idols of men,
women, birds, animals, and things that crawl. That would be the trade
only a fool would make. They began to treat themselves and other created
things as God should be treated.

Therefore God gave them over in the lusts of their hearts
to impurity, [so] that their bodies would be dishonored
among them. For they exchanged the truth of God for a
lie, and worshiped and served the creature rather than the
Creator, who is blessed forever. (Romans 1:24–25)

There is another if-then statement here. If God's people decide to give
up the glory of God for an idol, then He will give them over to impurity
and dishonor. Unfortunately, many humans are willing to accept that
trade. As a result of this horrible exchange, mankind begins worshiping
what was made rather than the one who made it. This is part of the process
of searing the conscience. The outcome of this searing is eternal separation
from the Father.

For this reason, God gave them over to degrading
passions; for their women exchanged the natural function
for that which is unnatural, and in the same way also,
the men abandoned the natural function of the woman
and burned in their desire toward one another, men with

men committing indecent acts and receiving in their own
persons the due penalty of their error. (Romans 1:26–27)

If now man and woman have reached the condition in verse 25,
meaning if they exchanged the truth for a lie, what is at the bottom of
this downward spiral? The answer to that question is a depraved mind.
The spiritual battle is in the mind, and the outcome is in the flesh. One
can only observe that if all humans made this choice, reproduction would
cease. In one generation, mankind would be extinct. There would be no
physical reproduction.

And just as they did not see fit to acknowledge God any
longer, God gave them over to a depraved mind, to do
those things which are not proper. (Romans 1:28)

Verse 28 and verse 21 are bookends for this process. Verse 21 addresses
people who do not honor or thank God. Verse 28 says those people did not
see fit to acknowledge God any longer. If and when we reach the depraved
mind condition, God will allow us to self-destruct rather than rescue us.
A person does not need to be rescued from a situation that has a beautiful,
divine way out. Jesus is that way. We need not stay broken. We can find
the way and be saved. Even in this seared condition of depravity, God loved
us. God's love is not performance based.

The difficulty in discerning between good and evil in the preceding
account illustrates how diluted our today's Christian worldview has
become. The next paragraph is an example of how easily we slip.

There is a historic process for finding underground water. It has been
used for generations. From what I have been told, it works something like
this. A person takes a forked stick or tree branch that is Y shaped and holds
the two prongs of the Y in his hands. He then walks slowly, and when
he passes over where there is underground water, the stem of the Y will
point downward. I understand that wire can be configured in such a way
as to duplicate the outcome. The process is called "water witching," and
the forked stick or wire is called a "divining rod." On different occasions,
I have met evangelical pastors and elders who say it is okay for believers
to practice water witching. The fact that they use the term "witching" for

the process, and the tool used is called a "divining rod" is explained away as a bad choice of words. They say it is okay because "it works." Yes, our Christian worldview has become diluted, twisted, and polluted. When we say anything is okay because it works, we are in a dangerous ditch. When we use God's approach, we win every time. When we try to go to the same place where God took us before but do it without God, we lose every time. Satan is imitating without the power and without holiness. The predictions may be accurate, and the outcomes may sometimes work, but the process can and will be disastrous.

Next we have the New Testament account of Paul's encounter with someone who is doing the same thing as the lady with whom King Saul met years before—fortune telling.

> It happened that as we were going to the place of prayer, a certain slave-girl having a spirit of divination met us, who was bringing her masters much profit by fortune-telling. (Acts 16:16)

There is a demonic spirit of divination. Divination is defined as the practice of attempting to foretell future events or discover hidden knowledge by occult or supernatural means. One of the manifestations in this instance is fortune-telling, the act or practice of predicting the future.

My wife and I were blessed to have raised our first two children (daughters) in a farm home built by my great-grandmother. She and her husband emigrated from Scotland in the early 1850s. Her husband died in his early forties. He left his widow when the youngest of their seven children was a baby. My great-grandmother was smart, semiliterate, and industrious. Family oral history says she was in charge. She put together a rather large farm, and in 1869, three or four years after her spouse's demise, she finished building the home in which we found ourselves living a hundred years later. The home had four bedrooms (three upstairs and one downstairs). When our daughters were old enough to sleep through the night, we put each of them in their own bedrooms upstairs while we remained downstairs.

With alarming frequency, our oldest girl would show up at our bedside, telling us that there was a person in her room. She didn't seem frightened but was not very happy about it. In the beginning, my wife would get up and take her to the place of the alleged person sighting to show our daughter that no one was there. I had slept upstairs all my life and was certain no one was ever in my room. After several years and many repetitions of this scene, we would send her back upstairs, telling her there was no person hanging around the house. This must have become as discouraging for her as it was for us. She got so she would come downstairs and silently stand by the head of her mother's side of the bed. We would be sound asleep, and she would stand there until her mother sensed her presence. When this happened, there would be a loud scream from her mother. It was a scream that would effectively wake me and frighten away any person who was intruding.

At this stage of our life, we were what our denomination called "churched"; and being churched was about all there was to Christianity. We went to church but were ignorant of the spiritual world and had no clue about salvation. When the Lord did capture us, we were exuberant new Christians but unwilling warriors. Our two daughters received Christ at that time as well. They were ten and eleven years old. God made it clear we were going to be warriors, and He didn't need our approval. He just needed our obedience.

About this time, my brother began exploring family history. One of the discoveries of his research was that our great-grandmother missed her husband so much that she had held séances in the new house. She built the home immediately after her husband died. He had never lived there, and she was understandably alone. Perhaps she was even frightened.

We realized there was a high probability that our ancestors had opened the door to spirits who were not holy. We vacated them with the name of Jesus. Years later, as young adult Christians, the girls, along with their four-years-older aunt, begin telling us about how they used to spend time playing with those "people" in the walk-in attic of the old home. Thirty years later, they still affirm this experience.

Our oldest daughter continued to have experiences with the enemy into adulthood. I asked her to relate her final experience. This happened after she was married and had several children. The spiritual headship had changed, but the spiritual war continued. She and her husband were active in a soul-winning, Bible-teaching teen ministry in Waterloo, Iowa. The following is her account of their victory.

> *My earliest memories include seeing and playing with people who I know now to be demons. They were always dressed in long, dark clothes. I was never afraid and didn't think anything was strange about them. They just always were [there].*
>
> *It was shortly after we moved to Waterloo, Iowa, in 1981 that they began to reappear. Roger [my husband] did not see the man that came to our trailer but always knew when he was there. I saw him, and he spoke to me. He looked like Rumplestiltskin with green clothes on. He always asked if he could see our children, and when I said no and commanded him to leave in the name of Jesus, he left. The interesting thing about this demon is that he must have been a "familiar" demon. Years later, my neighbor began to tell me the same story about a man appearing in their trailer asking to see her children. I asked what he looked like, and she described the man I saw exactly—down to his top hat and pointy shoes.*
>
> *I continued to see demons for years, and they became more and more aggressive toward me. God was doing a work through our lives in the Waterloo community, and many were coming to Christ, so I have to wonder if we had become a threat to Satan; therefore, the greater manifestations.*
>
> *I was sick on a Sunday morning in the early 1990s, so I stayed home from church and went to bed. Prior to this, we often heard unexplained footsteps in the house, doors opening and shutting, and both recognized demonic presence frequently. I didn't see demons as often but was [frequently] paralyzed by them so I couldn't move. Sometimes at night I could even feel the warmth of my husband's hand next to mine and yet wasn't able to touch it. Roger would have times where he felt like something was sitting on his chest and he couldn't breathe.*

This time I was lying in bed and heard footsteps coming up the steps. I tried to move but couldn't. The steps stopped beside the bed, and I saw the shadow of a hand on the ceiling of my room. I tried to speak the name of Jesus but couldn't. The hands came around my throat and choked me until I passed out. When I came to, I saw the shadow of the hands coming down again. I was able to say "Jesus," and they stopped. I just repeated the name of Jesus, then "in the name of Jesus," then "in the name of Jesus, I command you to go." [I said this] over and over until I was able to move again. I prayed for the Holy Spirit to replace where the demons had been, and then such a peace filled our home that I fell asleep. That was my last encounter. I went to a Jim Logan seminar about spiritual warfare and later learned about how to break the generational ties.

I am not certain how or why she did not get set free and stay free from generational spiritual activity when the rest of us were set free. She did, however, come to know that she could be set free and accessed that freedom forever.

Discussion Topics from Unit 17

According to 1 Timothy 4:1, what spirits and what doctrines are dangerous?

What will they cause?

When will they cause it?

According to 1 Samuel 28:7, what did Saul tell his servants to do?

What was Saul's purpose for this?

According to Acts 16:16, what did the servant girl do that made money for her owner?

Unit 18

Discernment and Aid

I relay my daughter's experience with spiritual warfare to make it clear that the same spiritual behaviors are triggered today as were in Saul's time.

A spiritualist was contacted. Spirits were invited into the home by great-grandmother's efforts to reach the dead. Those spirits were still there with great-grandmother's descendants a hundred years later.

Saul didn't have the name of Jesus and the delegated authority to deal with them. We had that authority, and we used it to evict them. They left. They stayed gone. We are not under the law; we are under grace. We are not under the curse; we are under the blessing. Today that snare is broken (see Psalm 124). If people allow ungodly spiritual activity to impact their lives, it is because of their ignorance, innocence, or invitation.

One of the prayer warriors of our fellowship often said that we Christians love to take our demons to church with us. Unfortunately, we dislike someone else's demons, but we seem to think ours are going to be fine.

There are ways we can resolve this dilemma of not being able to identify an evil spirit, or enjoying fellowship with a spirit we know is evil. The help needed can be found in 1 Corinthians 12:8–10. It will reveal some resources God has provided to ensure victory in Jesus.

> To one there is given through the Spirit a message of wisdom, to another a message of knowledge by means of the same Spirit, to another faith by the same Spirit, to another gifts of healing by that one Spirit, to another

> miraculous powers, to another prophecy, to another
> distinguishing between spirits, to another speaking
> in different kinds of tongues, and to still another the
> interpretation of tongues. (1 Corinthians 12:8–10 NIV)

When we find ourselves struggling with spiritual dilemmas, we need help. We need to get the spiritual help God has made available for us. We need to learn to possess and practice those various tools He has made available to us.

In this instance, the spiritual gift of discernment or distinguishing of spirits is an effective help. Rely on that gift for a first investigation of a spirit. A second help is to find someone who is spiritually mature and seek his or her input. Third, try or test the spirits. See if the spirit in question confesses Jesus Christ. This should become a natural practice in our quest of holiness. We certainly cannot expect a high degree of holiness in our lives or the lives of our family if we have a bunch of Satan's imps running around in our attic. Get them out of there! Test those spirits! Evict the demonic ones in the name of Jesus.

> Beloved, do not believe every spirit, but test the spirits
> to see whether they are from God, because many false
> prophets have gone out into the world. By this you know
> the Spirit of God: every spirit that confesses that Jesus
> Christ has come in the flesh is from God; and every spirit
> that does not confess Jesus is not from God; this is the
> spirit of the antichrist, of which you have heard that it is
> coming, and now it is already in the world. (1 John 4:1–3)

These first three verses are primer on how to be certain you are correctly reading a situation. They start with a warning about false prophets in the world. Obviously God is telling John that He wants false teaching weeded out. He tells us in simple terms how to make the determination.

> You are from God, little children, and have overcome
> them; because greater is He who is in you than he who is
> in the world. (1 John 4:4)

John discusses the empowerment we have received. He tells us that we, though we are little children in God's eyes, have been able to overcome the spirits from the antichrist. The reason He gives is that the God, who is in us in the form of the Holy Spirit, is greater than the "god" who is in this world.

> They are from the world; therefore they speak as from the world, and the world listens to them. We are from God; he who knows God listens to us; he who is not from God does not listen to us. By this we know the spirit of truth and the spirit of error. (1 John 4:5–6)

What we say is critical to a successful walk with God. Jesus asked Peter, "Who do you say I am?" Jesus was and is the same—then and now. Who do you say He is?

Listen carefully to your teachers and preachers. Who do they say He is? They will probably echo Peter's correct response, because they know it. If so, then what do they teach? Do they say Jesus came that we might have life and have it abundantly? Do they say God is going to pour out His wrath upon us if we don't meet His standards, or do they say Jesus bore all of God's wrath for us? Who do they say Jesus is? Do they say Jesus gave the only possible perfect sacrifice for sin, or do they say our job is to perfect his sacrifice through our behavior? Saved people can positively or negatively impact their lives by their confessions. Our confession of the Word is crucial to living life as an overcomer.

Many church people can talk about the Lord or talk about God but are unable to talk about Jesus Christ. There are people who only use His name as a swear word.

Nearly always, the person who doesn't use the name of Jesus has no relationship with Him. Those people are candidates for conversion. Through what is said and what isn't said, they reveal that they don't know Him. It is what they don't say that gives them away. That is an example of testing the spirit. Spirits will reveal in some way that a person is a candidate for conversion! Not being comfortable using the name of Jesus is one way people reveal that they don't know Him. It might be considered testing the spirits.

First Corinthians 2 introduces us to a spirit. This is one spirit we all get exposed to in large doses—the spirit of the world.

> What we have received is not the spirit of the world, but the Spirit who is from God, so that we may understand what God has freely given us. (1 Corinthians 2:12)

We have a big "S" Spirit in this verse, along with a little "s" spirit. The former is, here, as always, the Holy Spirit. The latter is the spirit of this world. Verse 12 tells us which of the two spirits will reveal that it is not from God. When red flags go up, stop and get out of there. One of the purposes of this series is to acquaint us with what is clear cut, good, and evil, and point out danger areas.

First John told us to test the spirits we encountered. We're instructed to do so by asking: does the spirit being tested confess Christ?

When I say, "confess Christ," I mean, do the words and actions a spirit is presenting agree with the written Word of God? Does the Holy Spirit in you agree? Does your born-again Christian fellowship agree? The totally dependable one of these is the first. If the Word says it is sin, then human opinions to the contrary are wrong.

> But having the same spirit of faith, according to what is written, "I believed, therefore I spoke," we also believe, therefore we also speak. (2 Corinthians 4:13)

We have looked at two Bible-identified spirits. First Corinthians told us there is a spirit of the world, and 2 Corinthians tells of a spirit of faith. What do the verses describing the spirit of faith and the spirit of the world have in common? What could either spirit say that would convince you to do or not do something? Does either of them confess Jesus to be who He said He is? Does either of them say things that agree with the written Word?

> Here is a list of the things each of the spirits is saying.
> What has the spirit of the world been saying to you?

The spirit of the world says:

> "Everyone is doing it."
> "Do whatever it takes to keep your job."
> "Have sex with whomever you please."
> "It is okay to badmouth political or other leaders."
> "It is all about me."
> "I am my own person."
> "Husbands should have control of their wives."
> "There is no God."
> "No one will notice."
> "You are not capable of this."
> "People can sin so badly that God won't forgive them."
> "Submission is stupid."
> "We evolved."
> "This planet just happened."

The spirit of faith says:

> "Separate yourselves from them."
> "Do all things as if you were doing them for Christ."
> "All sex outside of marriage is sin."
> "Leadership is given by God."
> "It is all about Him, not about you."
> "You and I were purchased with a very high price."
> "Husbands should be ready to die for their wives as Christ was ready to die for His Church."
> "In the beginning, God created."
> "God knows my coming and going."
> "I can do all things through Christ who strengthens me."
> "Minister to the poor."
> "Minister to the afflicted."
> "Minister to the widows, orphans, and brokenhearted."

This same spirit of faith convinces us that while we were yet sinners Christ died for us. What has the spirit of the world been saying to you? Satan's workers never tell us anything that agrees with God's Word.

However, everything the spirit of faith tells agrees with His Word. One spirit is a liar, one tells the truth. Who are you hearing? Who are you believing?

As we discuss how to discern spirits, it is important to also study how spirits manifest themselves in the realm where we live and function. First Samuel offers some insights into the spirit realm.

The following account from 1 Samuel focuses on a woman named Hannah. Hannah was one of two wives of a man. The other wife was having children while Hannah was barren. She was constantly belittled by society and her competitor. Eli, the priest, observed her behavior in the sanctuary as she wept and moved her lips without sound. He accused her of being drunk, but she explained that her behavior was responding to the Spirit.

> But Hannah replied, "No, my lord, I am a woman oppressed in spirit; I have drunk neither wine nor strong drink, but I have poured out my soul before the Lord." (1 Samuel 1:15)

Hannah knew her problem was one of being "oppressed" and not "possessed." The distinction? In the spiritual realm, being oppressed is leaning on and trying to change a direction, while being possessed is about total and complete control of a demon over a person.

Oppress: to crush or burden by abuse of power or authority, to burden spiritually or mentally, weigh heavily upon.

When Hannah said she was oppressed, she was saying she had a burden to do what she knew was not pleasing to God. She was wise enough to go to God for help.

Satan never wants us to go to God, though. He wants us to be out of control. He wants us to make decisions that will separate us from God. He doesn't need to have possession of our will. He can oppress us enough to lead us into sin.

Hannah correctly diagnosed the problem and the solution. She was oppressed, so she went to God. She had made a covenant with Him. She was speaking in her heart when Eli discerned something was wrong.

Spiritual oppression can impact nations. Spiritual oppression can last for centuries. Genesis is a good place to find an example.

> God said to Abram, "Know for certain that your descendants will be strangers in a land that is not theirs, where they will be enslaved and oppressed four hundred years." (Genesis 15:13)

Oppression, as it is used here, has the connotation of slavery, of being enslaved. When it comes to Satan, he always wants control. He wants us in his workforce. Unfortunately, the wage in his workforce is death. Remember that the descendants of Abram were not captured by Egypt. They made a choice and lost contact with the lordship of their God. The oppression in this case did require a deliverer to set them free.

In spiritual oppression, not everyone whose story is told in the scriptures was happy with being delivered. In Hannah's case, she went to God and pleaded for her delivery. God responded to her wishes.

Not all the Hebrews were as happy when their deliverance came as Hannah was with hers. When the Hebrews left Egypt, they murmured and complained. Many said they were better off in slavery. The book of Acts has a brief account of what that oppression was like.

> And when he saw one of them being treated unjustly, he defended him and took vengeance for the oppressed by striking down the Egyptian. (Acts 7:24)

This describes the state of oppressed people, saying they were "being treated unjustly." This is an account of how Moses responded when he saw a captive being abused. Micah 6:8 says acting with justice is good in the eyes of God. All satanic activity is exactly the opposite of what God endorses. Satan is referred to as the "angel of darkness," but he can copy. He can disguise himself as an angel of light. Jesus considered the oppression of people to be one of the focuses of His earthly ministry.

> The Spirit of the Lord is upon me, because He anointed me to preach the gospel to the poor. He has sent me to proclaim release to the captives, recovery of sight to the blind, to set free those who are down-trodden [oppressed]. (Luke 4:18)

Jesus considered that this satanic condition of oppression put His people in need of deliverance and healing as surely as the blind needed sight and the poor needed to hear the gospel.

Discussion Topics from Unit 18

According to 1 Corinthians 12:10, which one of the gifts of the spirit specifically mentions spirits?

According to 1 Corinthians 2:12, why have we been given the Spirit of God?

According 1 Samuel, what is the enemy spirit doing to Hannah?

According to Luke 4:18, what was Jesus's ministry for the oppressed?

According to Nehemiah 4:17, why were those people working with one hand?

Unit 19

Earthly Ramifications of Temporary Rule

Satanic activity will harass Christians from every angle and at every opportunity. Two of these that I am comparing and contrasting are the spirit of oppression and the spirit that possesses or controls an individual. Unit 18 concluded with a description of oppression. Now we look at what the Word says about possession. The account of the demonic in Mark 5:1–13 dramatically illustrates demon possession.

> They came to the other side of the sea, into the country of the Garasenes. When He got out of the boat, immediately a man from the tombs with an unclean spirit met Him, and he had his dwelling among the tombs. And no one was able to bind him anymore, even with a chain; because he had often been bound with shackles and chains, and the chains had been torn apart by him and the shackles broken in pieces, and no one was strong enough to subdue him. (Mark 5:1–4)

The first four verses describe the physical manifestations of a person possessed by an unclean spirit. This incident happened before the cross, before the empty tomb, and before the Holy Spirit was loosed on earth. This controlling spirit is identified as "unclean." The first characteristic listed in this account is the superhuman strength of the man so possessed. He appeared as man in a horror movie from the twenty-first century. The reader of this account can almost see him running, flexing his muscles, screaming, and growling at anyone he encountered.

> Constantly, night and day, he was screaming among the tombs and in the mountains, and gashing himself with stones. Seeing Jesus from a distance, he ran up and bowed down before Him; and shouting with a loud voice, he said, "What business do we have with each other, Jesus, Son of the Most High God? I implore You by God, do not torment me!" (Mark 5:5–7)

Verses five through seven describe the spiritual, mental, and emotional manifestations that may appear in spiritual possession. The presence of the Son of God was a torment for him. This was a man in tremendous agony. This empowering, possessing spirit knew and obeyed the protocol for approaching the Son of God. He bowed down and addressed Him by His appropriate title. He asked for grace from Jesus, saying, "Do not torment me." The appearance of Jesus Christ on the scene transformed the tormentor into the one who was tormented.

The demonic appears to have the ability to create more havoc than Samson of the Old Testament could create on a good day; in spite of those strengths, the scripture records no account of him injuring anyone other than himself.

> For He had been saying to him, "Come out of the man, you unclean spirit!" And He was asking him, "What is your name?" And he said to Him, "My name is Legion; for we are many." (Mark 5:8–9)

This is one of the verses that led me to believe that there are many different physical manifestations of the spirit identified as unclean. The passage starts out describing the man as someone with an unclean spirit. This is not problematic to the believer; the outcome of the encounter was going to be the same, regardless of name or number. There are teachers of deliverance who use these verses to teach believers that we need to know the name of the perpetrating spirit. My experience is that if there is a need to know the spirit's name, God will empower you to discern it. Refuse to allow a conversation with a demon. You have nothing to discuss. You are the one in the position of power.

> And he began to implore Him earnestly not to send them out of the country. Now there was a large herd of swine feeding nearby on the mountain. The demons implored Him, saying, "Send us into the swine so that we may enter them." Jesus gave them permission. And coming out, the unclean spirits entered the swine; and the herd rushed down the steep bank into the sea, about two thousand of them; and they were drowned in the sea. (Mark 5:10–13)

Jesus is Lord! Everything in the universe is under His control. Luke recorded for us another instance of Jesus dealing with a demon. All wondered at the power and the message. There is unmistakable irony when the Son of God sends spirits that are called unclean into animals (swine) that were listed as unclean. The imagery is awesome.

> And amazement came upon them all, and they began talking with one another saying, "What is this message? For with authority and power He commands the unclean spirits and they come out." (Luke 4:36)

Who should be more amazed—the people who saw this happen under the direction of the incarnate Messiah, or we who see it today through the power of His Holy Spirit? He did it with a command. We do it with a command and the delegated authority of His name! All should be amazed.

A definition of "possessed" is someone who is influenced or controlled by an outside source. Throughout history, one source of control can be demonstrated by an addiction to a substance. The following verse gives an Old Testament view of what possession is. It has not changed much in thousands of years. Possession says, "I own it, it is in my hands, it is mine."

> I bought male and female slaves and I had homeborn slaves. Also I possessed flocks and herds larger than all who preceded me in Jerusalem. (Ecclesiastes 2:7)

This verse from Ecclesiastes can be viewed as a biblical definition of possession. Possession has a sense of "being owned by." A person's will at his death may say something like, "I leave all my earthly possessions to so and so. I own these things, I possess them, they are mine, and I will do with them as I please. Even in death, I will control them." So it is in the spirit realm: a person truly possessed by a spirit (good or evil) has surrendered control of his or her life to that spirit. My opinion is that those people may not know they are doing it, but often they are aware that an activity they are engaging in is dangerously evil.

Were the people we just read about in Mark 5 intimidated? Yes, they were! Should they have been intimidated? Yes, they should have been. Why should that have been the case? The residents of this region were living in the same fallen spiritual state as the demonic. None of them may have been under as strong satanic control as this guy, but they did not have the spiritual or physical power or authority to protect themselves from the havoc he was capable of creating. Here is another spiritual irony. The one person in the universe who could help them was there. His name was Jesus, and they ended up asking Him to leave. The gospel according to Matthew has another account of possession.

> When evening came, they brought to Him many who were demon-possessed; and He cast out the spirits with a word, and healed all who were ill. (Matthew 8:16)

Obviously, demon possession was not unusual at the time of Christ. I wonder why. One can speculate that since this was before Pentecost, before the outpouring of God's Spirit, perhaps the demonic world was less constrained than it was after Jesus's victory at the cross. The cross hadn't happened. The empty tomb hadn't happened. The risen Christ had not happened. Those happenings greatly reduced Satan's power in this world.

The next few verses give clues as to how Satan can and will manifest himself through spiritual attacks. If he is allowed to win the attack, possession is the outcome. All the following verses clearly state what can happen as the result of possession.

> As they were going out, a mute, demon-possessed man was
> brought to Him. (Matthew 9:32)

This person lost speaking skills. Can stammering, stuttering, and muteness be symptoms of spiritual activity? Sometimes. Have we tried to remedy physical manifestations of spiritual problems with man-designed therapies? Sure we have.

Do you remember the original curses after Adam and Eve sinned in the garden? They involved pain in childbirth, weeds in the crops, and sweat and diseases in food production. When righteousness went away, these things came in. That hasn't changed either. When a person has not accepted God's righteousness, it results in difficulties in every phase of life. Man's response has been to turn to science (his intellect) rather than seek righteousness. We have developed painkillers, weed killers, ditch fillers, garden tillers, and we continue to struggle. We still have weeds. We have pain and a medicine chest to go with it. We have speech therapists, physical therapists, mental health therapists, and respiratory therapists. I suspect we may have therapists for therapists.

We have tilled the soil and had babies for thousands of years. For thousands of years, we have fought the curse. Have we gained victory? No. Why not? Where is the victory? In Jesus, when we find the righteousness of God, we will have found the victory. Victory is not in our heads or our intellect. Nor is it in the physical abilities of our hands. It is not in our skills and our talents even though those things are gifts from God.

Jesus is where the victory is now. Take a look at John 10:10. In this verse, Jesus clearly states that He came so that we could have eternal life, full and abundant—physical life that starts at birth and a victorious spiritual life that starts when we receive Him as who He is. I compare His victory to those month-long Amtrak passes where you can go anywhere for a month. The ride may not be what you expected, but it will get you where you want to be. When the price is paid, it seems wise to possess the product. Abundant eternal life! The price is paid!

> Then a demon-possessed man who was blind and mute
> was brought to Jesus, and He healed him, so that the mute
> man spoke and saw. (Matthew 12:22)

In this verse, the demonic manifestation also includes blindness. Certainly this says the manifestation of physical blindness can be a result of demon possession. Is all blindness caused by spiritual activity? According to this verse, sometimes that is the case; just as certainly, that is not always the case. In a broader sense (that Satan is "god of this world" at this time), yes—there will be the opportunity for dysfunction in our current body. When we pray "thy kingdom come on earth as it is in heaven," I'm pretty sure none of us are expecting to see people feeling their way along the streets of gold using white canes! We were instructed to pray asking for conditions here to be as they are in heaven. Jesus would not have given us that prayer if it were not possible. The same is true with "deliver us from evil." We have been told by our Lord to ask for deliverance or protection from evil. We are aliens here, but we do not have to be subject to any of the evil possibilities.

> In the synagogue there was a man possessed by the spirit
> of an unclean demon, and he cried out with a loud voice,
> let us alone. (Luke 4:33)

Demons do not want and will object with venom to the presence of a Jesus-loving, Bible-thumping, Spirit-filled sister or brother of Jesus. Demons don't have the right or authority to object, but they will, and we can tell them to shut up and get out. How? Through the name of Jesus—that is the name that has been given all authority on heaven and on earth and everywhere in between.

We have looked at some of the relationships and interactions we can and will have with the spirit realm. We will encounter that realm because God is Spirit. We were created in His image. We are spirits, we have souls, and we live in bodies! Our spirits are eternal. We have looked at the Bible and listed Spirits who are able to empower us, working hand in hand with us and with God. And we have looked at evil spirits and how they work hand in hand with Satan and with us to empower us to fail. Their goal is to disempower us. In the next unit, we will look at some biblical examples of what those spirits look like in action.

Discussion Topics from Unit 19

According to Matthew 8:16, were there many demon-possessed people in the area?

What did Jesus use to cast them out?

What percent of the sick were healed?

According to Luke 4:33, where was that demon-possessed man found?

According to Acts 7:24, what kind of treatment of a person or nation is symptomatic of oppression?

Unit 20

Deceit and False Doctrine

> Then a spirit came forward and stood before the LORD
> and said, "I will entice him." (1 Kings 22:21)

"Entice" is not a commonly used street word in twenty-first-century America. It is, however, a highly developed technique in marketing. It is a way to convince a person that he or she desires something.

Have you ever heard professionals practicing enticement? Of course you have. Every commercial is an effort to entice us into purchasing a product. It may be for some tempting snack specifically designed to get a person off a diet. Yes, that is enticing. It might be for a new car that is irresistible. Enticing spirits seem to be in control of our marketing system in the world. "Ya gotta have it!" they scream. "It will be rewarding," they promise. The world uses enticement to sell everything from good books to bad-smelling cheese.

That is a brief example of what enticing is in the marketing world. It is a professional effort to tempt us into a decision. What does enticement look like in the Bible? It looks exactly like it does in the world. Being able to lie, accuse, and deceive is an advantage for the person doing the enticing. Satan did a masterful effort at enticing during the temptation of Christ.

> Then Jesus was led up by the Spirit into the wilderness to
> be tempted by the devil. (Matthew 4:1)

The temptation of Jesus was round one of spiritual warfare after Christ was baptized and received the Holy Spirit. For the first time since sin entered the world, God was establishing a new presence on earth. During this conflict, Satan revealed several strategies that he still uses. He also demonstrated the powers he had before he was humiliated at the cross.

The enemy will look for a potential weakness or vulnerable areas of your life. Jesus, during His earthly years, was fully man and fully God. Verse 2 sets up the enticement in the fully man arena. Men get hungry. The human body makes a good case for the need to have some nourishment.

> And after He had fasted forty days and forty nights, He
> then became hungry. (Matthew 4:2)

This verse identifies the area of attack—this is, after all, called spiritual warfare for a reason. Satan knew of the power of hunger, and he decided to exploit it.

> And the tempter came and said to Him, "If You are the
> Son of God, command that these stones become bread."
> (Matthew 4:3)

Satan knew full well this was the Son of God. He would not have been nearly as concerned about anyone else who was walking the earth at that time. He starts the conversation with the word "if." The start of that conversation sounds a lot like his opening with Adam and Eve. He starts out questioning what God has said and done. We can be totally sure that Satan knew what God said when Jesus was baptized. It is recorded in Mathew 3:17; we all can know He is the Son of God. Enticement presents itself as a practical, viable solution to the perceived situation. Raise some doubt, relabel the situation, and define a way out.

> But He answered and said, "It is written, 'Man shall not
> live on bread alone, but on every word that proceeds out
> of the mouth of God.'" (Matthew 4:4)

Jesus counters and wins with the Word of God! He is quoting scripture. The victory is His. Like us, He found that there is always another battle following the current one. Like Jesus, we must persevere—being alert every time we win. We can be confident that we will win every time because Jesus won the ultimate battle. That old lion that I call toothless, clawless will be prowling around trying to talk us into death until Jesus arrives in the flesh again. It would be sad to let him gum us to death or maul us to death by enticing us.

What is the enticement in verse 5 of this passage?

> Then the devil took Him into the holy city and he had Him stand on the pinnacle of the temple and said to Him, "If You are the Son of God, throw Yourself down; for it is written, 'He will command His angels concerning you'; and 'on their hands they will bear you up, so that you will not strike your foot against a stone.'" (Matthew 4:5–6)

They're going through the same process all over again. This sure looks like a bad choice from the start. If you were going to entice the Son of God, would you consider it rational to try it on the pinnacle of His Dad's house in God's chosen city? Again, he (Satan) starts the dialogue with the word "if." Satan is even quoting God as being in favor of the ploy. When these things are happening to us, those are the times when we must know more than His Word. We must have a clue what it means.

What is the enticement here? It is to prove in human terms that Jesus really is the Son of God. Satan wants Jesus to prove it by doing superhuman or supernatural things. It seems to appeal to human ego. In God's way of doing things, when the time came for Jesus to perform His first miracle, it was because His mother told Him to do so.

> Jesus said to him, "On the other hand, it is written, 'You shall not put the Lord your God to the test.'" (Matthew 4:7)

Jesus is modeling for us. Jesus counters and wins with the Word of God! He is saying it. He is quoting it. We can and should do the same thing. The victory is His. He correctly divides the Word. Jesus makes it look easy. Satan doesn't give up easily though.

Again, the devil took Him to a very high mountain and showed Him all the kingdoms of the world and their glory; and he said to Him, "All these things I will give You, if You fall down and worship me." (Matthew 4:8–9)

We looked at these verses earlier in the study. At that time we were looking at Satan being the small "g" god of this world, as well as examining the powers he had before Christ's death and resurrection. These two verses point out some powers he had. He had the ability to instantly and safely transport humans (Jesus was fully human at this time) anywhere in the world. He had the power to give away kingdoms. Jesus was not impressed. The dialogue continues.

Then Jesus said to him, "[Go], Satan! For it is written, 'You shall worship the Lord your God, and serve Him only.'" (Matthew 4:10)

Neither should we be impressed. We have the same Word, and we have the authority because He gave us that authority. We need to possess it and practice it.

Then the devil left Him; and behold, angels came and began to minister to Him. (Matthew 4:11)

This verse clearly reminds us that those ministering angels were held back as Jesus sweated blood for us in the garden. He was serious when He said He could call in legions of them for help, but He chose not to. They were held back as He withstood the shame and torture of the crucifixion. Those were the battles He had to win alone. Then He gave the victory to us.

What does it look like when you get several demonic spirits influencing a man? The next passage is lengthy.

But Gehazi, the servant of Elisha the man of God, thought, "Behold, my master has spared this Naaman, the Aramean, by not receiving from his hands what he brought. As the Lord lives, I will run after him and take something from him." (2 Kings 5:20)

Through this passage, we will see the collaboration of several satanic spirits as Gehazi allows them to persuade him to sin. The battle always starts in the head, and if thoughts in our head go unabated, they can ruin a life as they did in this account. Gehazi is lied to, and unfortunately he likes the lie. Sometimes we like the lie! In this case, the lie is that his boss, Elisha, has made a mistake, and it is his responsibility to correct it. Gehazi has been lied to and deceived. His response will be to lie, deceive, and steal. All of those errors were decisions made by the servant of a man of God. Gehazi lost the spiritual battle in his head then he lost the battle in the flesh.

> So Gehazi pursued Naaman. When Naaman saw one running after him, he came down from the chariot to meet him and said, "Is all well?" He said, "All is well. My master has sent me, saying, 'Behold, just now two young men of the sons of the prophets have come to me from the hill country of Ephraim. Please give them a talent of silver and two changes of clothes.'" (2 Kings 5:21–22)

Gehazi's opening three words, "All is well" were the only words of truth in the exchange. It is well for us to remember that he is the one being led by an enticing spirit. The enticement is to cash in as much as possible from this encounter. In today's language, he is a con man.

> Naaman said, "Be pleased to take two talents." And he urged him, and bound two talents of silver in two bags with two changes of clothes and gave them to two of his servants; and they carried them before him. When he came to the hill, he took them from their hand and deposited them in the house, and he sent the men away and they departed. (2 Kings 5:23–24)

What a grand plan with a grand outcome in Gehazi's eyes. He not only got the goods but he got someone to carry it for him. He thought the witnesses left the scene as well.

> But he went in and stood before his master. And Elisha
> said to him, "Where have you been, Gehazi?" And he said,
> "Your servant went nowhere." (2 Kings 5:25)

"Where have you been?" That could have been God's question of
Adam and Eve after they hid among the trees in the garden. In the present
time, as in past times, sin begets sin, and Gehazi lies to cover his lies.
Elisha was a man whose eyes had been opened to the spiritual world. This
had been made evident when he asked God to allow his servant to see the
protection they had, and God revealed the band of angels to Gehazi. Old
Testament times or today, the Spirit of God (the Holy Spirit) will reveal
the truth.

> Then he said to him, "Did not my heart go with you, when
> the man turned from his chariot to meet you? Is it a time
> to receive money and to receive clothes and olive groves
> and vineyards and sheep and oxen and male and female
> servants?" (2 Kings 5:26)

Are we going to make a business of God's gifts? This is a temptation
that seems to be common in today's Christian. There is nothing wrong in
receiving gifts. The wrong comes in an attitude of heart that thinks it is
okay to lie and deceive for the purpose of receiving gifts. That is stealing!
Real people of God proclaim His Word and perform their ordained
ministries because they love Him and they love His people.

> "Therefore, the leprosy of Naaman shall cling to you and
> to your descendants forever." So he went out from his
> presence a leper as white as snow. (2 Kings 5:27)

Enticing spirits know our weakness at the moment. They know our
willingness to justify our actions. Mr. Old Enticing is usually accompanied
by a few of his friends, lying spirits. Yes, there are deceitful spirits, and there
is demonic doctrine. All three of them have the goal of killing, stealing,
and destroying.

> But the Spirit explicitly says that in later times some will
> fall away from the faith, paying attention to deceitful
> spirits and doctrines of demons, by means of the hypocrisy
> of liars seared in their own conscience as with a branding
> iron, men who forbid marriage and advocate abstaining
> from foods, which God has created to be gratefully shared
> in by those who believe and know the truth. For everything
> created by God is good, and nothing is to be rejected if it
> is received with gratitude; for it is sanctified by means of
> the word of God and prayer. (1 Timothy 4:1–4)

What does a deceitful spirit look like in the world?

I have a story that I think demonstrates what a deceitful spirit looks like today. After the first day of a training I was attending, the facilitator went out with a few of us for the evening meal. There were three or four of us, and we shared about families and backgrounds to pass the time. The facilitator shared with obvious pride how he recently had taught his eleven-year-old son how to sneak popcorn into a movie theater without getting caught.

That is a deceitful spirit. What had he taught his son? Did he teach him that sneaking, lying, and cheating to save the price of a bag of popcorn was okay? God told us that we need to be faithful in the small things first. What happened with that boy is just the opposite of what God's Word requires and is sinful.

Being deceitful or following a deceitful spirit is lying with intent. The intent from the beginning is to deceive. It is knowingly making false statements, being deliberately untruthful. It is a false statement made with deliberate intent to deceive—a falsehood. In the hierarchy of the genre, it is a cut above just plain not telling the truth. It is the royalty of conning.

During my tenure of working with the chronic intergenerational unemployed, one of my clients was a forty-something mother living in small apartment with her seventh-grade daughter. Her son was in a state prison for violating substance abuse laws. The father of her children was in a federal prison with a long time to serve for violating federal substance abuse law.

I met with her monthly from February through June. I did not connect as well with her as I was accustomed to doing. She treated me with respect. She mechanically did what needed to be done. When we were closing a meeting, she would frequently say, "I am so thankful I am no longer doing street drugs." Being a good counselor, I would affirm that confession. When I arrived for the July home visit, her presence was different from before. She was saying angry things about her neighbors and anyone else that came to mind. Finally, I asked if there was any chance she had overmedicated. Her daughter, who was not in her mother's view, emphatically nodded her head yes.

It turns out this lady who was so proud of being off street drugs was abusing prescription drugs. That involves conning the doctors, conning the pharmacist, and conning the Department of Human Services. She later shared her drug history. She had been through detox ten times. One of the detox facilities was Christian, and she had made a commitment there. However, she was aware when she told me she was proud of being off street drugs that I was hearing that she was drug free. She was also convinced she had not lied to me. That is a deceitful spirit at work. She was lying to herself as well as everyone else. The good news about this person is that she recommitted to Christ, went through one more detox, and ten years later was still sober and holding down a decent job.

The deceitful spirit is not honest, and it is not genuine. Deceitfulness intends to charm and gain trust, intends to be misleading, and intends to perpetrate fraud. Deceitfulness has developed lying to an art form. It can couch a lie in a self-created and perhaps a self-believed illusion. Deceit is hollow, empty, without character, and smooth.

One of the skills practiced by lying spirits or deceitful spirits in the process of conning or enticing their victims is to get into the victim's value system and worldview. Evangelical Christians, because they have made their value system and worldview known for hundreds of years, are prime hunting for them. They will use scripture to make their case, just as Satan did while tempting Jesus. They can fake repentance superbly with crying and anguish like hired mourners of another age.

> Now therefore, behold, the Lord has put a deceiving spirit
> in the mouth of all these your prophets; and the Lord has
> proclaimed disaster against you. (1 Kings 22:23)

Deceitful spirits seem to be common among addicts, including those addicted to domestic violence. You must be a con to get away with it. Often the male perpetrators in homes where I worked made sure they had established a strong rapport with the local police. They had them conned.

You must be able to believe the lie before you can spread it. Because of the content of this lesson, I want to make sure everyone knows what I am talking about and what the Word says about the gospel. Let's look at it the way Paul wrote it. Then we will move on to the application.

> Now I make known to you, brethren, the gospel which I preached to you, which also you received, in which also you stand, by which also you are saved, if you hold fast the word which I preached to you, unless you believed in vain. For I delivered to you as of first importance what I also received, that Christ died for our sins according to the Scriptures, and that He was buried, and that He was raised on the third day according to the Scriptures and that He appeared to Cephas, then to the twelve. After that He appeared to more than five hundred brethren at one time, most of whom remain until now, but some have fallen asleep; then He appeared to James, then to all the apostles; and last of all, as to one untimely born, He appeared to me also. (1 Corinthians 15:1–8)

Paul saw the Word of God as the truth. Our walk with Him today requires that same unswerving adherence to the Word. He said this biblical prediction of a resurrected Messiah was verified by hundreds of people. Many people saw him die, and many saw the risen Savior. He is saying that the fact that Christ's death and resurrection were foretold in the Bible validates the truth of Jesus Christ. The gospel as Paul lays it out here is that Jesus died for our sins, and He rose from the dead. Paul repeated the phrase according to the scriptures to give absolute authority to the statement.

> For by grace you have been saved through faith; and that not of yourselves, it is the gift of God; not as a result of works, so that no one [may] boast. (Ephesians 2:8–9)

To use Paul's words in introducing more commentary, I should say "according to the scriptures." According to Ephesians 2, the means to receive the gift of God requires using the same level of grace that caused Him to pay the price of redemption in advance. There is nothing we can do to get ourselves saved. The Word of God tells us it is all done. It is important to have a handle on the truth as we look at what Satan puts up as the truth. He has some sorry imitations he and his dark spirits are trying to sell.

> But the (Holy) Spirit distinctly *and* expressly declares that in latter times some will turn away from the faith, giving attention to deluding *and* seducing spirits and doctrines that demons teach through the hypocrisy *and* pretensions of liars whose consciences are seared (cauterized), who forbid people to marry and [teach them] to abstain from [certain kinds of] foods which God created to be received with thanksgiving by those who believe *and* have (an increasingly clear) knowledge of the truth. For everything God has created is good, and nothing is to be thrown away *or* refused if it is received with thanksgiving. (1 Timothy 4:1–4 AMP)

When someone who claims to be leading in the name of Jesus makes statements that say you must or you cannot do certain things, we need to have the Bible in our hands and the Holy Spirit indwelling. A lying or deceitful spirit wants control. As he did in the temptation of Jesus, the enemy will use scripture to entice us. He just won't use it the way God intended; he'll reverse it.

A deceitful spirit is of the same genre as the lying spirit, only more sophisticated. They are shameless and slick. People who choose to listen to them take on the same characteristics.

Paul tells Timothy, in verse 1 of chapter 4, that the Holy Spirit is without question telling him what he is writing to Timothy.

> But the Spirit explicitly says that in later times some will fall away from the faith, paying attention to deceitful spirits and doctrines of demons. (1 Timothy 4:1)

Theologians call this falling away "apostasy," as if it were a thing that happens to some believers. In this verse, Paul says it happens to people by listening to deceitful spirits. People who choose to listen to and promote unscriptural doctrines are choosing to join the wrong army.

What kind of things are you going to hear when you are being taught by someone who is "giving attention to deluding and seducing spirits and doctrines that demons teach"? Each thing you hear will be the opposite of what God wants. What will happen to you? You will be deluded and seduced by the enemy.

> I am astonished that you are so quickly deserting the one who called you to live in the grace of Christ and are turning to a different gospel—which is really no gospel at all. Evidently some people are throwing you into confusion and are trying to pervert the gospel of Christ. (Galatians 1:6–7 NIV)

In his letter to Timothy, Paul talks about falling away to follow deluding and seducing spirits and doctrines that demons teach. In his letter to the Galatians, he uses a different name. When he talks about it here, he changes his approach. He tells them they are deserting "Him who called you by the grace of Christ, for a different gospel." Paul uses a military term here. He, in my paraphrase, calls it deserting to the enemy (for a different gospel).

That is an outcome of deceitful doctrine fostered by what Paul told Timothy was "giving attention to deluding and seducing spirits and doctrines that demons teach." If you do those things, you will have deserted to the enemy.

Paul says these teachers are disturbing you and want to distort the gospel of Christ. Isn't that exactly what lying and deceitful spirits will try to do? They want to confuse, distort, and twist the truth. When it comes to his presentations, Satan has a verbal house of mirrors.

Most of us have seen examples of mirrors designed to make people appear taller, smaller, rounder, or thinner. They are designed to distort, and when we see ourselves in one of them, we laugh. We laugh because we know the truth. The deception is so far away from the truth we find it to be humorous. There is nothing funny about Satan's deceptions. They are intended to mislead us—to steal from us, to separate us from God, and ultimately, to kill us. Knowing the truth renders them a harmless irritant rather than a fatal poison.

When preaching or teaching seems to distort issues and disturb you, it is an example of a deceiving doctrine.

> But even if we, or an angel from heaven, should preach to
> you a gospel contrary to what we have preached to you,
> he is to be accursed! (Galatians 1:8)

Paul is serious about this. He says that even if an angel preaches or teaches something different from those basics we looked at in 1 Corinthians, that person is accursed. It is important when making a statement to be able to say as Paul did, "according to the scriptures." Ending up cursed is what happens to anyone adhering to "giving attention to deluding and seducing spirits and doctrines that demons teach."

> As we have said before, so I say again now, if any man is
> preaching to you a gospel contrary to what you received,
> he is to be accursed. (Galatians 1:9)

He repeats the curse again. One of my spiritual mentors was a member of a local small-town church. One Sunday, the pastor preached a sermon during which the pastor taught seven things one needs to do to be saved. My friend took notes. He reported to the church's district superintendent what had been taught and supported it with his notes. The district superintendent responded that the position taken by the pastor was not even Christian. The doctrine of the denomination with which the local church was affiliated taught that one is saved by grace through faith and even the faith is a gift from God. He did not choose to take any action against the pastor. He was willing to have what he accepted as heresy taught rather than perform the duties of his office and correct the error. When we hold to values like that, can the heathen tell us from the world? The answer is absolutely not.

If you are hearing a message similar to the one my friend heard, one that distorts issues, or if you see a church official refrain from disciplining such a teacher, you should be disturbed about that. Be sure you are protected. Know as simply and precisely as possible what the gospel is, so that when it is perverted, you will not even be tempted to abandon the path you have decided to follow.

But who is the one listening to deceitful spirits? A person can only fall prey to untruths when he does not know the truth. We looked at Satan trying to entice Jesus with lies and deceitful doctrine, but it was of no avail. It didn't work! Jesus took it one step further. He not only knew the truth but He is the truth! Protection is clearly available from the Word.

Is protection from bad doctrine available from teachers of the Word? Maybe. But maybe is not close enough when the outcome could result in being accursed. I suspect that every one of us who teaches gets it wrong sometimes. But protection from biblical teachers is not what Paul was talking about. He was talking about listening to demons and allowing them to mess with our minds.

Do we learn the truth from experience? Perhaps in certain circumstances that is the case, but the experience needs to be correctly appraised! While I was serving on a local school board, one of the senior teachers resigned. I said to the superintendent, "That is too bad. That teacher has twenty years' experience." The superintendent replied, "No, he has one year of experience, but he has had it twenty times." God has given us the tools to correctly evaluate experience. Tools aren't helpful if we refuse to use them because we don't like the results they bring.

Do we gain protection from the Holy Spirit indwelling and empowering us? Yes, we do, every time. Correctly connected to experience and teaching, along with the indwelling Holy Spirit, we can be quite safe from the teaching of deceitful spirits and doctrines of demons.

The goal of this book is and has been to acquaint us with the spiritual realm. God's Holy Spirit is an inexhaustible and empowering stand-alone topic on which we have not touched. I have limited the teaching to spirits that can be found listed by name in the *New American Standard Bible*, or on occasion the *New King James* or *Amplified Bible*.

I want to start out this section with a review of what I consider two out of the four key scriptural concepts the believer needs to grasp to be comfortable and confident in the area of spiritual warfare during his or her walk with the Lord.

1. 1 Corinthians 15:1–8: A clear understanding of the gospel; it is vital for all believers to understand this world-changing truth.
2. Ephesians 6:10–18: This scripture supplies a list of the armor we need when engaging the enemy, which, by the way, is all the time.
3. Colossians 2:13–15: This verse, along with the following Ephesians passage, iterates the total victory Jesus accomplished in His part of the war with Satan. He won! The devil may roar around like a lion seeking to devour us, as Peter said in his letter. He will, however, be roaring around with no teeth and no claws.
4. Ephesians 1:20–22: According to Ephesians 1:20–22 and Colossians 2:13–15, Jesus completely disarmed Satan at the cross and at the empty tomb. Satan has to fight the battle in our heads, getting us to empower him as Adam and Eve empowered him in the garden. Paul apparently worried about this as well. He specifically mentioned this danger in his second letter to the Corinthians.

> But I am afraid that, as the serpent deceived Eve by his craftiness, your minds will be led astray from the simplicity and purity of devotion to Christ. (2 Corinthians 11:3)

The serpent deceived Eve by his craftiness. Because of his ability to entice, he was able to steal their dominion over planet Earth. They decided to believe his words rather than God's words. Our minds can be led astray or deceived by the same craftiness. It is clear in this verse that even in the beginning, Satan worked in people's minds. He convinced us to give him power beyond what God intended, and it seems we are happy to give it to him. Satan, through his craftiness, continues to accuse and deceive mankind. He gets away with this primarily because we do not use the tools we have been given to win our part of the battle. Now is the appropriate time for us to use them. There is not much need for those tools after we die, but there is a need while we live.

I recently heard an account of the young man who bought in to a demonic doctrine. My paraphrase of the incident is as follows. The doctrine was simple in its content. The teacher was presenting to a group of people. He said that if a person would pray for a fatal illness, and if, along with that request, prayed that death would glorify God, God would grant both requests. A young man who was in attendance decided he was going to do this. The young man, to his knowledge, was perfectly healthy. Within days, he was dead of leukemia. Strangely, some people did get saved. A second person who had attended the meeting and who knew of the death passed an account of this happening to his girlfriend. She decided to do it as well. She died within a few days. These were young people!

Jesus said in John 10:10 that he came so that we might have eternal life and have it abundantly. It is not hard to discern that this teaching is the opposite of what Jesus taught. Satan was able to kill two people by having someone teach them the doctrine of demons. It is the opposite of the truth.

Another incident of which we have firsthand knowledge involved an acquaintance from a neighboring town. She was familiar with the miraculous work God was doing through the local group of believers. She announced with no medical support or evaluation that she had a brain tumor and was going to die from it. She was adamant that none of us pray about her or her illness. We were not obedient to her wishes; we prayed. Within a few years of confessing the brain tumor and separating herself from believers, she did have one, and she did die from it. The first couple of years of her confession of cancer, doctors could find no sign of a tumor. She accepted a lie—a deceitful doctrine—and it culminated in her untimely death. Who is it that wants you dead? Who comes to kill steal and destroy?

> "For I have no pleasure in the death of anyone who dies,"
> declares the Lord God. "Therefore, repent and live."
> (Ezekiel 18:32)

God wants us alive. The doctrine of demons wants us dead. These people were lied to, and the results were fatal. The unseen arena of spiritual warfare can have very real, very visible, physical outcomes. The battle is in the brain! We make a conscious decision. We say, "This makes sense to me. I'm going to do it." We make the decision! That settles it.

I had a great friend work with me on the farm. He and I worked together for eight years without a disruptive disagreement. Frequently, when I would come up with a question or suggestion about how a job should be performed, he would respond with a silly grin, saying, "It makes sense to me." I could be sure when he responded that way that the plan needed some changes.

When Satan starts conning us, he wants us to use our heads; he wants us to sincerely say, "It makes sense to me." When we accept an offer from him, we have sold out our world to him as surely as Adam and Eve sold out their world to him.

There are deceitful spirits, and there are demonic doctrines. Just because a teaching or doctrine seems to make sense does not make it correct and acceptable. These false teachings often come so close to the truth that each of us must know the truth well, or we will be swept off our feet by the winds of doctrine.

My wife and I once attended a Bible study in which the teacher chose to explain each scripture by either an historical context or a social context. He was using intellectually accepted secular facts as a method to prove scripture. I cannot pretend that scripture is less accurate than history or social conditions of the time. Those things often help frame a correct view or understanding of scripture but should never be allowed to discredit what the Word contains. I would refer the reader to a book, *Evidence that Demands a Verdict* by Josh McDowell. He very logically compares the accuracy of scripture with the accuracy of historical accounts from the same time period. He found without exception that historical accounts are impacted by revisionist thinking and errors of transcribing, so a current account of an historical happening often will vary significantly from the original manuscript. The same tests applied to scripture found very little variation in the accounts. Attempting to use the mores of several thousand years ago to explain why God said or did something is even more suspect. We don't need a non-scriptural explanation of why something is recorded in the Bible if it is also explained in the Bible.

In verse 2 of 1 Timothy 4, Paul tells Timothy how the transfer of dominion from God to Satan takes place. He tells us how solid believers get led astray. This is another insight into spiritual warfare.

The Spirit clearly says that in later times some will abandon the faith and follow deceiving spirits and things taught by demons. Such teachings come through hypocritical liars, whose consciences have been seared as with a hot iron. (1 Timothy 4:1–2 NIV)

As it is used here, the word "hypocrisy" means the same as our definitions of lying or deceit. It is the practice of lying with intent. It was no accident that the people whom Paul was addressing were teaching wrongly. The deceitful spirit is handing the lie to them, as he does to us, on a satin pillow of intellectual or historical reasoning. We begin to reason that hypocrisy is truer than scripture. That is when the searing takes place.

Searing is a method of sealing off the surfaces of something so that it won't respond as it was designed to respond. Some people like to throw their steaks on a super-heated grill, leave it for a couple of seconds, and flip it over—searing it so the juices stay in. People with severe nosebleeds sometimes have to have the source of the bleeding seared to stop the bleeding. In those examples, searing is good. The searing talked about in Timothy is a sealing off of the conscience, so it no longer reacts to various stimuli as it should. The hot iron used to seal off the conscience is lies.

When branding livestock with a heated iron, their first reaction is one of pain and discomfort, and the cows will fight to get away from the branding iron. After the initial contact, the nerve endings are seared, and the animal will no longer fight it. When our conscience tells us a doctrine or teaching is a lie, we will fight it at first, but repetition and continued listening to the lie will eventually ease our discomfort. We will be seared.

Even gradually accepting lies allows deceit to sear our conscience. Gradual acceptance disables our ability to discern God's path for us. His truths become blurred. We can't be followers without a path, and we can't discern our path with blurred vision. A conscience that is not functioning because it has been seared by continued exposure to and acceptance of lies is not simply blurred vision; it is spiritual blindness.

We are the ones who make the decision that allows this to happen. Suddenly the path of Jesus has become hidden from our vision. Without a path, we all will most surely fall away.

Discussion Topics from Unit 20

According to Ephesians 2:8, we are saved by what?

We are saved through what?

According to Ephesians 2:9, what would happen if the above answer were not true?

According to Galatians 1:8, what happens to someone who teaches or proclaims an incorrect doctrine?

According to John 14:16, what or who will God give us?

Unit 21

The Doctrine of Demons

The outcome of listening to or paying heed to the doctrines of demons is failure. It is talked about again in 1 Timothy 4.

> Men who forbid marriage and advocate abstaining from foods, which God has created to be gratefully shared in by those who believe and know the truth. (1 Timothy 4:3)

A common arena of spiritual activity concerns baptism. Satan loves to stir up trouble on this subject. I am sure many readers can relate accounts where born-again believers fell out of fellowship with each other over this issue. Infant baptism, adult believer baptism, sprinkling, immersion, or pouring will not raise my ire. People can and do have sound doctrinal stances on all of these. Satan can and will take advantage of those honest differences. He will destroy human relationships over this. That is wrong. That is hurtful to the kingdom. The reason I will not enter into a divisive discussion over this is because I know Holy-Spirit empowered Christians on all sides of this issue. My loving advice is to get into the love chapter (1 Corinthians 13) and read it out loud a few times.

I want to point out what it looks like when a doctrine of demons gets its hands on the issue. I have a very dear friend who was raised and saved in the Baptist tradition. He was saved, and baptized by immersion. He would correctly preach it and teach scripture. One day, he ran into a denomination that said he was not saved because he was not immersed in the right direction or not immersed enough times. He was mature enough in his faith and knowledgeable enough in scripture to leave, shaking his head.

Another way the enemy tries to distract from the celebration of salvation is to convince believers that a person's salvation is dependent upon the words the baptizer says while performing it. Those teachings tie salvation to how you were baptized. Romans 10:8–10 ties our salvation to our hearts and mouths. John 1:12 ties our salvation to receiving and believing. Ephesians talks about grace, faith, and free gifts.

One danger concerning this issue is the danger of neutralizing a believer. These teachings can and will break earthly interpersonal relationships. They can also weaken and confuse a believer's relationship with God. Satan is trying to get a believer weakened in his faith, thereby getting that person off the battlefield. If I am questioning my enlistment in the army, then I will not make a very good soldier.

When the decision to buy into one of these doctrines is made, we transfer power to the enemy as surely as Adam and Eve transferred dominion in the garden. When they decided the serpent's point was valid, that it made sense to them, they acted on their decision. They accepted the doctrine of demons. Yes, they were dealing with the boss demon, but that makes him no more powerful. They were walking in the presence of God until this happened.

There truly is much of this kind of teaching. There are Old Testament diets, Daniel diets, and cleansing diets being pushed by both secular and Christian groups. Certainly a diet may be healthy for some people, or perhaps all people. But if someone tells you that we must follow it or suffer dire spiritual consequences, it has become a doctrine of demons.

It is not at all uncommon to see a TV preacher interviewing a person presenting eating "musts" for living long and well. What does the very next verse in 1 Timothy 4 say?

> For everything God created is good, and nothing is to be
> thrown away or refused if it is received with thanksgiving.
> (1 Timothy 4:4 AMP)

Give thanks for it, eat it, bless it, and digest it. The great commission verses, as set forth in the sixteenth chapter of Mark, talk about being protected from all sorts of dangers when we are walking with the Lord, proclaiming Him and loving Him. When Jesus sent out men to minister in his name, He told them to eat what was set before them (Luke 10:7).

There are groups who call themselves Christian who endorse gay marriage as well as heterosexual couples living together without the benefit of marriage. Those principles are the doctrines of demons pushed by Satan's minions. They are promoted by lying and deceitful spirits and accepted because people have not believed the truth and ended up with their conscience seared, having been led astray. They, in turn, lead many more into their condition.

Satan is not operating from a base of power. He is not going to overcome us with strength. The tools he has left will only work if we furnish power for them. He can only attack and win if we make the choice to allow it. He is crafty. He is patient. Sometimes we do not recognize patient and crafty for what they are, and we are enticed by them.

> [Jesus summoned His twelve disciples and] gave them authority over unclean spirits, to cast them out, and to heal every kind of disease and every kind of sickness. (Matthew 10:1)

A search of the word "spirit" in the Bible will find "unclean" to be the most commonly used adjective when talking about satanic spirits. Unclean seems to be a catchall word. All demonic spirits are unclean!

We have spent a lot of time examining what lying and deceitful spirits can do to the believer. Now we will look at them teaming up with a cohort.

> "It will come about in that day," declares the Lord of hosts,
> "that I will cut off the names of the idols from the land,
> and they will no longer be remembered; and I will also
> remove the prophets and the unclean spirit from the land."
> (Zechariah 13:2)

Now we have a different combination. In this verse, God is coupling idols and false prophets with unclean spirits! A deceiving spirit will want us to believe that false prophets, idols, and unclean spirits are good, or at the very least, that they are harmless. I was blessed with a special aunt who lived past a hundred years of age. She had been raised in a Methodist home and decided to convert to Catholicism when she was in her forties. She was a devout, faithful servant of the Lord and her fellow man. As age limited her activities, she spent hours assembling rosaries. She gave to the poor, ministered to the sick as she was able, but she always worked with her beads. I became concerned that I never heard her use the name of Jesus or say anything that would indicate she had a saving relationship with the Lord.

One day when she was in her late eighties, I asked her if she had asked Jesus to be her personal Savior. She rather huffily replied, "You know I have." I continued to press and ask her how I should know that. I had never heard her say anything that would indicate salvation. I didn't quit. The third or fourth time I pressed the issue, she said, "I have asked Jesus to be my Savior." My wife and I affirmed that and celebrated a little with her. The next time we visited her, she was working with her rosaries. We jokingly asked why she was doing that; her response was that she was doing it just in case. She had never allowed herself to live in the joy and contentment that comes from knowing that her works were fine, but it was Jesus who would get her to heaven. Her work did not appear to be from love but from fear. She had been misled by false prophets and unclean spirits, even though she was one with the Lord. When she died, she was buried with a rosary in her hand.

A biblical example of a sickness being caused by a spirit can be found in the book of Luke.

> And there was a woman who for eighteen years had had a
> sickness caused by a spirit; and she was bent double, and
> could not straighten up at all. (Luke 13:11)

This verse is an example of a spiritually perpetrated illness that was left nameless. Neither the spirit nor the disease was identified. The rest of this text makes it clear the fact the spirit had no name did not impact the outcome. The demonic spirit still lost. The victory has been won.

⌐Where are some spiritual battlegrounds? Big battles or small, where should we believers be focusing our prayers? Revelation 16 clearly identifies where a few of the major battlegrounds are.

> The sixth angel poured out his bowl on the great river Euphrates, and its water was dried up to prepare the way for the kings from the East. Then I saw three impure spirits that looked like frogs; they came out of the mouth of the dragon, out of the mouth of the beast and out of the mouth of the false prophet. They are demonic spirits that perform signs, and they go out to the kings of the whole world, to gather them for the battle on the great day of God Almighty. (Revelation 16:12–14 NIV)

"They go out to the Kings of the whole world." One of the battlegrounds involves world leaders, leaders in government at all levels. Twice in this passage, reference is made to signs. Abilities in the realm of magic, and imitating the signs and wonders done by the Holy Spirit, are still available to the demonic world. They use these in the war as tools to lie and steal. Leaders can be deceived into seeing events as Satan wants them to be seen. God tells us to pray specifically for these people (1 Timothy 2:1–2).

> Psalm 106:37
> "They even sacrificed their sons and their daughters to the demons."

The battleground is about human trafficking, child slavery. The battleground is about abortion. The battleground is about teaching a nation's children false religions. The list could go on and on. The war is about good and evil, righteousness and unrighteousness. It is about darkness and light. Once in power, a nation's leaders can take the people in any direction. God, in His Word, gave a very simple direction to us. He told us to pray for our leaders. Church leaders and people of power are not exempt from being misled.

I Corinthians 10:19-20

"What do I mean then? That a thing sacrificed to idols is anything, or that an idol is anything? No, but I say that the things which the Gentiles sacrifice, they sacrifice to demons, and not to God; and I do not want you to become sharers in demons. (1 Corinthians 10:19–20)

One of the most horrible actions taken in the name of God is human sacrifice. When this happens, Satan has accomplished exactly what he wants. This is when the killing part of his mission statement of killing, lying, and destroying is real. What about sacrificing our children by teaching them to worship the idols of today? Is it possible that something as cool as technology can become an idol? Education? Work? Glamor? Athletics or popularity? What kinds of pressures are being placed on parents to cave in to the whims of the current age? In 1 Corinthians, Paul says sacrificing to idols is sacrificing to demons. That is a serious charge; certainly it is a charge for which none of us want to stand judgment.

Discussion Topics from Unit 21

According to Mathew 10:1, Jesus gave His people authority over ...?

According to Zechariah 13:2, what are the three things God was going to remove from the land?

According to Revelation 16:14, where do the demons do their thing?

According to 1 Corinthians 1:20, to whom do Gentiles make sacrifices?

According to Philippians 3:9, where does righteousness come from?

Unit 22

Demons and Possession
More Battlegrounds

> And he cried out with a mighty voice, saying, "Fallen, fallen is Babylon the great! And she has become a dwelling place of demons and a prison of every unclean spirit, and a prison of every unclean and hateful bird." (Revelation 18:2)

The battleground is in the trade centers of the world. Babylon as used in scripture is often referring to the business of doing business worldwide. Right or wrong, our stereotype of people on Wall Street is that they are all wealthy. If and when they sell out to Satan, they have huge impact worldwide. Lucifer is an equal-opportunity destroyer. He is after our children. He is after the low income, those struggling in poverty; he is after the wealthy and those who can't possibly spend as much money as they have. Satan's goal is death for all. But he can only accomplish his goal if we (individually) allow it.

Yes, Satan has more than an ample number of soldiers in his army. There is not, however, a demon behind every doorknob, and they are not responsible for every bad thing that happens. Nor are they responsible for every behavior of which you or I might not approve. Demons can be found anywhere, as the following verses testify. They do not always possess (control the actions of) a person; they frequently oppress (exert pressure on) people from the outside. They can directly impact your thinking, or they can use a person to impact your thinking. Any media type, any form of communication, can and will be used.

We are talking about the battlegrounds. We Christians like to think the battleground is any place where we are not. Taverns, houses of prostitution, or halls frequented by politicians. However, these verses from Mark point us in a different direction.

> Just then there was in their synagogue a man with an unclean spirit; and he cried out. (Mark 1:23)

How do we know that demons can dwell in anyone? The verse above clearly points out that demons are capable of being in adult males.

The battleground is in our churches. We Christians do like to take our demons to church with us. What must Paul, in 2 Corinthian 13:5, have been thinking when he wrote the instruction for Christians to examine themselves? Psalm 26:2 and 1 Thessalonians 5:21 are two more verses stressing the importance of examining ourselves to see that were are continuing to follow the truth of Jesus Christ and His grace.

> And He [Jesus] went into their synagogues throughout all Galilee, preaching and casting out the demons. (Mark 1:39)

Demons were bringing the battleground to everyone's hometown, including Jesus's hometown. No place is exempt from Satan's plan of attack. Everyone is a target for the enemy in this war. Demons certainly are in our churches.

My wife and I were members of a small congregation in which there was a divisive, deceitful spirit. There was constant turmoil. It went beyond the norm of personality conflicts. The impact of this spirit was broad and appeared to be affecting a large portion of the congregation. One evening, a member of the congregation and his teenage son attended a Christian businessman's meeting. On the way home, they decided they should stop at the church and pray. Although they were excellent followers of Jesus, they would not have defined themselves as spiritual warriors.

The two men knelt down at the altar before the Lord. One of them asked God to remove whatever it was that was causing the problems within the church. At that moment, there was a loud noise in the immediate area that sounded like crashing. The following week, one couple left the church. Immediately, the historic problems were gone and did not return.

There is demonic activity in churches. To be in victory, we must be willing to accept that as fact, but we do not have to accept it. The battleground is all around us. The victory is in Jesus.

> But the man from whom the demons had gone out was begging Him that he might accompany Him; but He sent him away. (Luke 8:38)

Demonic activity is no respecter of person or position. If demons see an opportunity to separate a person from God, they will make an offer to the individual. When we see and understand as this man saw and understood the divine power Jesus has in the universe, we, like this man, should be begging to become His follower.

> Soon afterwards, He began going about from one city and village to another, proclaiming and preaching the kingdom of God. The twelve were with Him, and also some women who had been healed of evil spirits and sicknesses: Mary who was called Magdalene, from whom seven demons had gone out. (Luke 8:1–2)

This verse shows that they can also be in adult females. It could be said that Mary was full of them. Being set free from that bondage and from that influence must have been an incredible experience for her and for those who knew her. If we follow the scriptural trail of Mary, we find that she became an immediate and permanent follower of her Lord and her Savior.

> But after hearing of Him, a woman whose little daughter had an unclean spirit, immediately came and fell at His feet. Now the woman was a Gentile, of the Syro-phoenician race. And she kept asking Him to cast the demon out of her daughter. And He was saying to her, "Let the children be satisfied first, for it is not good to take the children's bread and throw it to the dogs." But she answered and said to Him, "Yes, Lord, but even the

dogs under the table feed on the children's crumbs." And
He said to her, "Because of this answer go your way, the
demon has gone out of your daughter." (Mark 7:25–29)

Finally, this verse shows that they can be in children.

These three examples have been of men, women, and children who clearly had demonic activity in them. To reiterate a position I put forth earlier, I am convinced there is not as much demonic possession now as there was before the cross and empty tomb. Demons are finding a more subtle approach now. Way back in Genesis, the serpent was described as being subtle. This subtle approach is oppression that can still produce disastrous results.

So what is a new believer, a person who recently decided to be a follower of Jesus, to do when confronted by a person who wants deliverance from satanic activity? Early in our newfound relationship with Jesus and the truth of His Word, we received a call from Betty, a woman in our fellowship. Betty asked for permission to bring a woman to our house to meet us.

At the agreed time, they showed up at our front door. As they entered our front door, Betty introduced her friend. We said, "Welcome." The new friend said, "You talk about demons, I am full of them." All we understood at this stage of our walk was that all the universe must respond to the name of Jesus. We sat those two guests down in living room chairs and asked Jesus to protect everything and everyone there with His blood. We laid hands on the guest and asked, "What?" A voice uttered one word. We commanded it to leave in Jesus's name. We weren't counting how many times this happened, but each time, in response to the one-word question, we heard a one-word response as the demons were lined up waiting to be forced out. When we no longer got responses, we asked Jesus to fill her with His Holy Spirit and ended the evening in prayer. She would later state that Jesus changed her life that evening.

Discussion Topics from Unit 22

According to Mark 1:23 or Mark 1:39, can you take your demon to church?

According to Luke 8:2, can a woman have a demon?

According to Luke 8:38, can a man have a demon?

According to Mark 7:25, can a child have a demon?

Unit 23

Casting Out Demons

There is a saying that "imitation is the sincerest form of flattery." Consider that saying in relation to this verse.

> John said to Him, "Teacher, we saw someone casting out demons in Your name, and we tried to prevent him because he was not following us." But Jesus said, "Do not hinder him, for there is no one who will perform a miracle in My name, and be able soon afterward to speak evil of Me. For he who is not against us is for us." (Mark 9:38–40)

These disciples were correctly acting in the name of Jesus. When the Word of God is correctly applied, it will work. It will work even when the recipient is ignorant of what is happening. There are programs helping addicts that apply biblical principles without giving credit to the source, the Creator.

In the passage above, Jesus demonstrates the power in His name by performing miracles as the result of the use of His name. We encounter another if-then statement. If a person performs a miracle in Christ's name, then that person will not soon speak evil of Him. What if a person is not correctly using the name of Jesus? What if they don't get that part right?

> But also some of the Jewish exorcists, who went from place to place, attempted to name over those who had the evil

spirits the name of the Lord Jesus, saying, "I adjure you by Jesus whom Paul preaches." Seven sons of one Sceva, a Jewish chief priest, were doing this. And the evil spirit answered and said to them, "I recognize Jesus, and I know about Paul, but who are you?" And the man, in whom was the evil spirit, leaped on them and subdued all of them and overpowered them, so that they fled out of that house naked and wounded. (Acts 19:13–16)

They were incorrectly using the name of Jesus whom Paul knew. That meant bad news for the sons of Sceva. These people were not only unaware of who Jesus was; they were also using second-hand information gathered from a Jewish exorcist. A Jewish exorcist was not a wise source from which to learn the power of the name of Jesus. There is a two-thousand-year collection of false teaching available to us today. There are many people misusing the name of Jesus. They are not getting beat up physically, but they are often in trouble in terms of mental and physical health as well as having relationship problems.

Jesus models His principles. He shows how it's done. When Jesus teaches a principle, there is frequently a demonstration of how to perform that principle.

When Jesus saw that a crowd was rapidly gathering, He rebuked the unclean spirit, saying to it, "You deaf and mute spirit, I command you, come out of him and do not enter him again." (Mark 9:25)

Jesus operated in the knowledge and assurance of His authority. Further investigation of this scripture will reveal that the spirit did leave and did not return. When we are doing His work, in His name, and doing it according to scripture, we can be assured of the same result.

But if I cast out demons by the finger of God, then the kingdom of God has come upon you. When a strong man, fully armed, guards his own homestead, his possessions are undisturbed. But when someone stronger than he attacks him and overpowers him, he takes away from him all his armor on which he had relied and distributes his plunder. (Luke 11:20–22)

What a powerful if-then statement this verse has: "If I cast out demons by the finger of God, then the kingdom of God has come upon you." The moving of the finger of God and the casting out of demons are events that happen in the kingdom. And who has the kingdom come upon? It has come upon the follower of Jesus. The believer has been blessed, the kingdom has been displayed to the world, and God has been honored.

This is what it is like when an unclean spirit is indwelling a human being. That demon guards his stuff. His stuff is his own house, which would be the body of the person. His possessions would be the soul and spirit of this person. Then look what happens when the name of Jesus comes to the house.

We attack the enemy in the name of Jesus. We overpower the enemy in the name of Jesus. In the name of Jesus, we strip him of his armor upon which he relied, and we return the stolen goods to the rightful owner.

We move the finger of God by the name of Jesus. It is vital for the believer to understand the power in God-given spiritual authority. Generations have been taught that they are nothing beyond saved sinners. Jesus is saying "I, by the finger of God, cast out demons." It is the finger of God that does the casting out. Who moves the finger? In this scripture, it is Jesus. We are going to look at what the Word says about you and me and God's finger as we move through this study.

When the unclean spirit goes out of a man, it passes through waterless places seeking rest, and not finding any, it says, "I will return to my house from which I came." (Luke 11:24)

This unclean spirit has been evicted. It is homeless. It is not a happy demon. It goes to a desert like place that has no place of rest for it. Then the demon addresses his former residence. He refers to it as "my house." He thinks he has ownership of it. He calls it his, and he vows to return. He will return to see what is going on there.

Victories need to be protected. The believer or nonbeliever who has received deliverance or healing needs to be aware that Satan will try to give it back. It will often be in terms of a physical twinge or desire to return to a habit. When that does happen, the person must be prepared to address it and verbally cast it down as a vain imagination. Rebuke the manifestation in the name of Jesus. Avoid a kneejerk confession that says, "its back."

> And when it comes, it finds it swept and put in order. (Luke 11:25)

What is he going to find in this house when he gets there? It will be cleaned in the name of Jesus. It will be in order through the name of Jesus.

> Then it goes and takes along seven other spirits more evil than itself, and they go in and live there; and the last state of that man becomes worse than the first. (Luke 11:26)

If no guard has been placed at the gate of a man's soul, if no other spirit was asked to fill the vacancy, that demon will move back immediately and bring his friends. The condition will be worse than it was at the beginning. The evil will have been reinforced.

He teaches us to guard our spiritual victories. Demons can consider people to be their homes. It takes a strong power to evict them from the premises. I have often asked a person, before praying, if he or she will receive a healing or deliverance. Sometimes people become so comfortable with their conditions that they want to continue in them. God will not violate their desires.

Learning to guard our victories is essential if we are to keep from fighting the same battles over and over. When we evict a spirit, we do it simply by telling it to leave in the name of Jesus. We then act to fill the vacancy that was just created. Usually we ask for the spirit of love, peace, and a sound mind. We as believers need to be offering spiritual and emotional support as well as counseling on how to hold the victory.

Discussion Topics from Unit 23

According to Luke 11:24, where does a spirit go when it is forced out of a person?

According to Luke 11:25, what does it do after being forced out?

According to Luke 11:26, if this is allowed to happen, what is the last condition of the person?

According to 1 Corinthians 12:7, why were the spiritual gifts given to the church, the body of Christ?

According to Romans 4:21, of what was Abraham sure?

Unit 24

Equipped for the Work

In the synagogue, there was a man possessed by the spirit of an unclean demon, and he cried out with a loud voice. (Luke 4:33)

The demon was yelling at Jesus, telling Jesus to leave him alone. Jesus told the demon to shut up and get out of there. Jesus teaches that demons won't hurt people in response to Him. There is no need for a believer to hold a conversation with the twisted representatives of the enemy.

God makes it clear that, through Jesus and His Holy Spirit, we have been equipped to do good works. We have been offered the Holy Spirit, one who is greater than any power on earth. He told us to go and do as He did. Jesus rebuked, cast out, and gave us authority to do the same. And Jesus told us the spirit world is subject to His name.

Jesus did not say, "When you find a demon, come and ask me, and I will remove it." He gave us the name and expects us to use it. God is showing us here what the weeds of the world are. He has shown us how to identify them and affirms the power He has given us to overcome.

Years ago, before weed killers became as effective as they are today, we would hire high school students to walk the soybean fields; we gave them the authority and responsibility to walk over every square foot of the field and remove every weed. They didn't come to us every time they found a weed—they removed it. So are we to be in our spiritual walk—across the face of the earth, we are to use the authority we have received and remove every spiritual thing offensive to our God. In essence, we are weeding His fields.

> But to each one is given the manifestation of the Spirit for
> the common good. (1 Corinthians 12:7)

I find this verse to be frequently ignored when a believer decides to be critical of the list of spiritual gifts. This verse clearly states that each believer (each one) is given a gift of the manifestation of the Holy Spirit. What is given here is a *manifestation* of the Holy Spirit, not the Holy Spirit. The Holy Spirit was given to the believer when the believer received Jesus as Lord and Savior. All of the gifts are for the common good. For the common good of whom? The individual believer and the church as a whole. The Holy Spirit was given for the body of Christ. The manifestations listed in 1 Corinthians 12 are given for the common good of all believers. I have taught in churches where gossip was acceptable, but any manifestation of one of these gifts was unacceptable. God said they are for the good of the whole body! That settles it. I addressed these biblical facts during my message. A byline to this is that I was never invited to teach to that part of the body again.

> For to one is given the word of wisdom through the Spirit,
> and to another the word of knowledge according to the
> same Spirit. (1 Corinthians 12:8)

My first serious introduction to this list of gifts was as an unbeliever. A young couple read them to us and then said, "If you could have any of these gifts but only one of them, which one would you choose?" Implicit in this question was the possibility that one might receive that gift. If that was true, then my view of the Bible and the faith was going to have to be transformed. Since I did not believe in supernatural healing, miracles, or a spirit realm, receiving any of those gifts was beyond my capability. Only God's abundant grace and mercy as displayed in the salvation experience could make these real in my life and in my world. Those things became real in the now, not just in the past or in the future.

> … To another faith by the same Spirit, and to another
> gifts of healing by the one Spirit, and to another the

> effecting of miracles, and to another prophecy, and to another the distinguishing of spirits, to another various kinds of tongues, and to another the interpretation of tongues. (1 Corinthians 12:9)

The list of gifts of the spirit from 1 Corinthians is a list of tools He has provided to us to empower us as we perform His work. Frequently, a believer is permanently gifted in one or more of these spiritual gifts. They and those around them know they have a specific gift. It may be wisdom, knowledge, faith, healing, doing miracles, prophecy, spiritual discernment, tongues, or interpretation of tongues. These are tools for the battle we wage. It is important to know in one's heart that verse 7 says they are all given for the common good.

When God leads us into a situation where we must know something, the Holy Spirit will empower us to know how to respond. We've talked about the tools. Now it's time to move to the power and authority. Luke contains an account of Jesus sending seventy people out to minister ahead of Him. When they returned, they brought this report.

> The seventy returned with joy, saying, "Lord, even the demons are subject to us in Your name." (Luke 10:17)

His name is supreme in the universe. Every knee must bow, and every tongue acknowledges His authority. All demons are subject to the name of Jesus. He is Lord.

> Behold, I have given you authority to tread upon serpents and scorpions, and over all the power of the enemy, and nothing shall injure you. (Luke 10:19)

Jesus spoke this specifically to the seventy he sent out. This list says He has given authority over several things, including power over the enemy. He delegated the same authority to all believers again in Mark 16.

> These signs will accompany those who have believed: in My name they will cast out demons, they will speak with new tongues. (Mark 16:17)

He said this to "those who have believed in my name." There are a great number of people going to heaven who will never experience the joy of either of these experiences. I think in most cases they have been misled by well-meaning teachers. I had a pastor tell me he would never pray for a healing because one person might get healed and another might not. I observed his ministry for some years, and I concluded that he had the same theory about salvation. He was reluctant to discuss the subject of salvation with anyone.

Verse 17 is a partial list of what those who have believed can do. I assure you those who have faith and have been given the appropriate spiritual gift can do them.

> Nevertheless do not rejoice in this, that the spirits are subject to you, but rejoice that your names are recorded in heaven. (Luke 10:20)

There is great joy in working for and with our Heavenly Father through the name of Jesus, His Son, and the power of Holy Spirit. Jesus said, in my paraphrase: "This is great and to be celebrated, but wait till you see the sequel. Then you will learn what rejoicing is about." In Matthew 10, God connects the power with the responsibility.

> Heal the sick, raise the dead, cleanse the lepers, and cast out demons; freely you received, freely give. (Matthew 10:8)

He made giving a part of our responsibility. This hardly sounds like a suggestion either. You have received healing and deliverance, you have received cleansing unto salvation, you have been set free from your demons. It has to all be free—how can you not give that gift to someone else?

There are verses affirming the victory we have been given and the commission we have been given scattered from cover to cover in the Bible. Here are just a few of them:

> … And to have authority to cast out the demons. (Mark 3:15)

This was said to the twelve disciples as Jesus prepared them for their ministry.

> And they were casting out many demons and were anointing with oil many sick people and healing them. (Mark 6:13)

This was the report about the twelve sent out and empowered to do God's will. When Jesus sent people to do a job, He always empowered them to complete the assigned task. We have been empowered, and we have been sent. We don't all have the same gift, but we have the same gift giver. We don't all have the same ministry, but we have the same minister dwelling in us.

> Truly, truly, I say to you, he who believes in Me, the works that I do shall he do also; and greater works than these shall he do; because I go to the Father. (John 14:12)

Success is assured! I believe in Him. I believe the works that He did. I believe even greater things should be happening because He is with His Father. Do you?

> [For the Father loves the Son, and shows Him all things that He Himself is doing; and the Father will show Him greater works than these, so] that you will marvel. (John 5:20)

The Father Himself is the source of authority. He is the one who is doing the greater works. We just need to believe Him and do what He says.

> "These signs will accompany those who have believed: In my name they will cast out demons; they will speak with new tongues; they will take up serpents; and if they drink any deadly poison, it will not hurt them; they will lay hands on the sick, and they will recover." So then, when the Lord Jesus had spoken to them, He was received up into heaven, and sat down at the right hand of God. And

they went out and preached everywhere, while the Lord worked with them, and confirmed the word by the signs that followed. (Mark 16:17–20)

Take one last look at verse 20. It says, "They went out and preached everywhere." The response of our Lord, Jesus Christ, the anointed Son of God, confirmed the Word with signs and wonders. We preach the Word. He does the rest.

The final if-then statement:

If we do as instructed,
then He provides the signs and wonders.

The victory is ours. This victory was bought and paid for with the blood of Jesus, the only son of the living God. We are called to live in His victory in this world. The heathens, the Gentiles, should be able to see the difference between us and them. We, on the other hand, should be able to show them the way to experience the difference.

He told us His strategies in His Word. He first modeled those strategies through Jesus Christ during those brief years He walked the earth in the flesh. He told us that if we walk His way, He will do the rest. He will surely bless you as you follow His path.

Discussion Topics from Unit 24

According to Luke 10:17, what were and are demons subject to?

According to Mark 16:17, what can believers do to demons?

According to Mark 3:15, you shall have ...... to cast out demons.

According to John 14:12, what kind of works should we be doing?

According to Mark 16:20, if we are doing the great commission, who confirms our work?

How or with what will He confirm it?

TRUE DIRECTIONS

An affiliate of Tarcher Books

OUR MISSION

Tarcher's mission has always been to publish books
that contain great ideas. Why? Because:

GREAT LIVES BEGIN WITH GREAT IDEAS

At Tarcher, we recognize that many talented authors, speakers,
educators, and thought-leaders share this mission and deserve to be
published – many more than Tarcher can reasonably publish ourselves.
True Directions is ideal for authors and books that increase awareness,
raise consciousness, and inspire others to live their ideals and passions.

Like Tarcher, True Directions books are designed to do three things:
inspire, inform, and motivate.

Thus, True Directions is an ideal way for these important voices to
bring their messages of hope, healing, and help to the world.

Every book published by True Directions– whether it is non-fiction, memoir,
novel, poetry or children's book – continues Tarcher's mission to publish works
that bring positive change in the world. We invite you to join our mission.

For more information, see the True Directions website:
www.iUniverse.com/TrueDirections/SignUp

Be a part of Tarcher's community to bring positive change in this world!
See exclusive author videos, discover new and exciting books, learn about
upcoming events, connect with author blogs and websites, and more!
www.tarcherbooks.com

TRUE DIRECTIONS
AN AFFILIATE OF TARCHER BOOKS

Printed in the United States
By Bookmasters